10 Contemporary Classical Guitar Solos

Larry Hammett

To access the online audio go to:
WWW.MELBAY.COM/30979MEB

Cover art by Warren Taylor.

WWW.MELBAY.COM

Preface

Fantasias Felinas is a collection of ten solo guitar works composed in what I feel is a completely refreshing and unique manner. Beyond the thematic Spanish title references to felines (used broadly here) and to their elusive, graceful, fragile, Zen-like qualities, no premeditated consideration was given to the compositional process. My only desire was to generally imitate their subtle, elegant, stealthy qualities. These pieces were mostly improvised and, ever so gently, shaped to give them a sense of completion. The challenge and enjoyment for me came from notating the huge sections of improvisation after the pieces were recorded. These pieces would have never amounted to anything if notation and forethought had come before they were recorded. While some of the pieces have a very simple, easy to recognize folk-like form and harmony, others are more abstract. With the exception of *El Gato*, there were no melodic, harmonic, or compositional elements designed to reflect specific movements, gestures, or other aspects of felines. Performers should feel free to make their own interpretations to that end, based on their own personal experiences. The process used to compose these works belies further analytical discussion; however, I felt compelled to speak generally about each piece and offer a few anecdotes and performance suggestions in the notes on pages 4 and 5.

Contents

Performance Notes

"Gatos Callejeros", titled "Opus 66" on the CD and "**El Fin de Novena Vida**" – These two pieces are the only ones in the collection that have a suggested story line. The first six measures of both pieces are the same material with some elegant harmonic additions added to the latter. At measure 7, they begin to go their own way. Placed at opposite ends of the album, they serve as metaphorical bookends. The first piece on the album, "Gatos Callejeros", represents a fully mature feline at the apex of its physical and mental life. Both sophisticated and refined in movement and in intellect, it is also beautifully uncomplicated. The last piece on the album, "El Fin de Novena Vida", represents the cat in the late stages of its life. Still the same feline with some clever new nuances to its usual graceful entrance, she is soon a bit lost and obviously discombobulated at times . . . nonetheless . . . . . still beautiful.

El Gato - The second piece on the album was the first composition of this collection and serves as the formal beginning. As mentioned in the preface, it is the only piece with a premeditated compositional element that depicts a chase between two young cats. Inspired by the opening of Joaquin Rodrigo's third movement to the *Concierto de Aranjuez*, the chase begins teasingly at measure 16 with liberal pauses indicated by breath marks in the score. It then becomes a full-on chase at measure 43 with a faster steady tempo.

La Gata - Placed second-to-last on the album, "La Gata", serves as a recap to the entire collection. Virtually identical to "El Gato", it is a little faster, higher in pitch (capo II) and abbreviated with tiny variations in harmony. As an informal recapitulation to the collection, it is an unusual reminder of where we formally started and is well received both on the album and in live performances.

Blue Manx - The mysteriously abstract opening to this piece is rich in color and space. While seemingly free from the confines of meter, quite the opposite is true. It has a very deliberate pulse and is precisely notated. With so much repetition, the subtle and deliberate shifting of note values, space, and time, help to keep it breathing and very much alive. With each new melodic theme comes other elusive rhythmic and harmonic variations that move the piece along. Finally, at measure 86, both the performer and the audience get a surprise in metric clarity from a refreshingly steady groove with a repetitive melody that is free from variation and mystery, taking us comfortably to the end of the piece.

Vals de la Gatita - This is one of my favorite pieces on the album. It starts off slow and then never goes anywhere. A friend once commented that "It just seems to keep starting over." After contemplating that view for a few seconds, I thought, yes, it does and it's also done. The introduction makes an oblique reference to Erik Satie's *Gymnopedies*, followed by a short, cascading melody leading to 8 measures of music that repeat with some ornamentation. The *vals* wanders haphazardly from one of the aforementioned sections to another and ends. Enough said.

Las Gatitas - Besides being a very easy tremolo piece in which the tremolo never leaves the first string, this piece has four points of focus that help it become everything it can be. After the opening harmonic statement, the first tremolo section should be played very deliberately, slow and legato. This will help set up the surprise double-timed repeat of the tremolo which should be very fast and light. Subtle volume swells and accelerandos during the tremolo will also add to the overall ambiance. The grace-noted double stops between sections should be very light with the grace notes themselves being quick, almost ghostlike. Lastly, many performers fail to see the pattern that occurs between the double stops that have grace notes and the double stops that don't. It's not arbitrary. Look closely and you will see a very precise pattern to the grace notes as they relate to the changing time signatures.

Purrrrrrr - This piece is a simple folk song in form and harmony. Nothing really needs to be said about performance except maybe play it as legato and relaxed as possible. Take your time. The only note of interest is that I composed the first eight bars one lazy afternoon looking at the mountains outside of Bozeman, Montana, where I was studying with Christopher Parkening. That was in 1981. I never wrote it down and never knew what to add to the first eight bars. I played those same eight bars from time to time for almost 40 years. When I was finishing this project, I thought of it, played it, and the piece just finished itself. It was truly a moment of genuine satisfaction that those eight bars would finally have a home and be heard.

Catnip - This is a playful piece that, on the one hand, explores simple organic possibilities of the campanella technique. This is a common technique of playing scaler passages by alternating stopped and open strings. The short, slow campanella phrases at the beginning grow longer and eventually morph into two voices traveling in opposite directions. After a repeat of the opening, there are several sections that mostly function as a harmonic resolution to the tension created by the campanella exploration. Other than a small reference to *Afro Cuban Lullaby* in measures 43 - 50, this piece is simply a collection of short organic ideas held together by their ability to happily coexist in a playful scheme.

El Tigre - Like "Blue Manx", the pensive abstract opening to "El Tigre" seems free from meter, yet again, quite the opposite is true. It is also very deliberate in pulse and is extremely well noted to that end. Its beauty lies in the minutia of rhythmic and harmonic detail. As most of the pieces share the same necessity for subtle rhythmic, melodic, and rhythmic nuances to offset the potential shortcomings of repetition, "El Tigre" is probably the most sophisticated to that end. An explanation of every melodic phrase that, on repeat, leaves out one sixteenth note or adds an extra duration to one note would be exhausting to write and read. If you want to play these pieces as they were intended, simply listen to the music with the score and familiarize yourself with the minute details.

Larry Hammett

Gatos Callejeros (Opus 66)

Capo II
6th string to D

Larry Hammett

Circa 𝅗𝅥 = 69

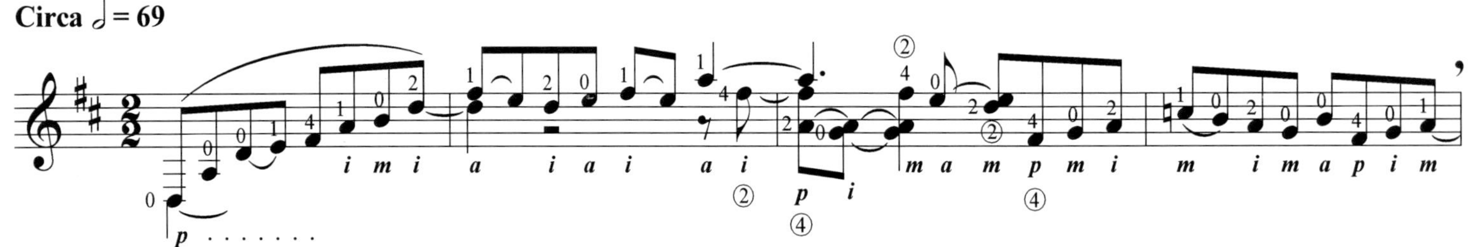

Measure 8, 1st time - poco rall. and breath mark / 2nd time - a tempo

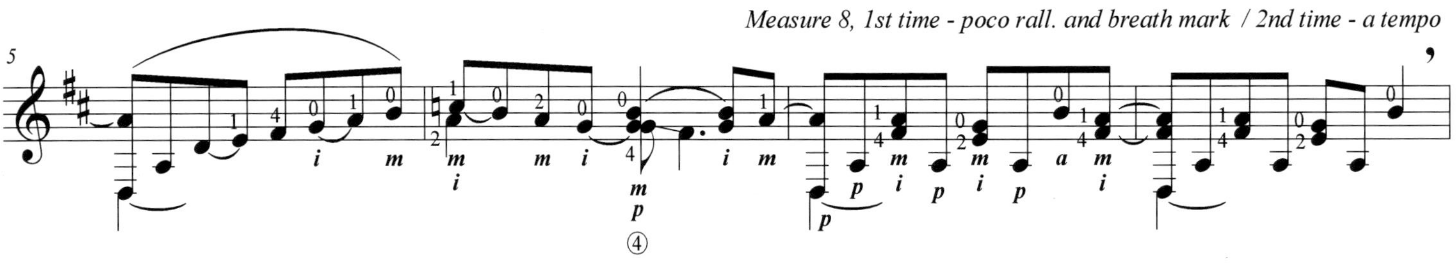

a tempo

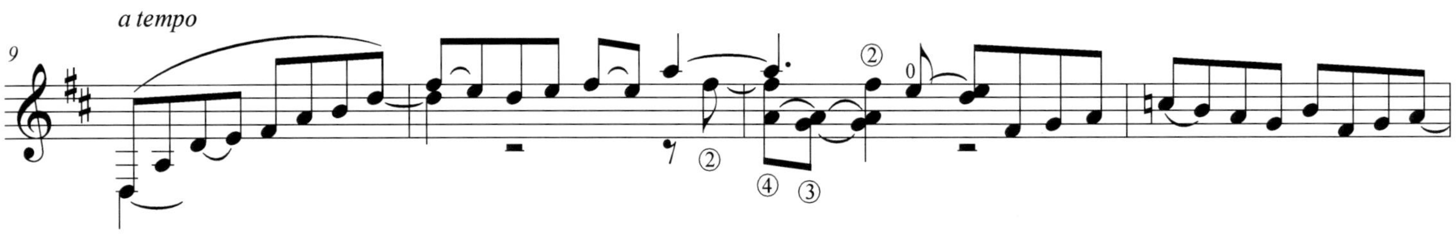

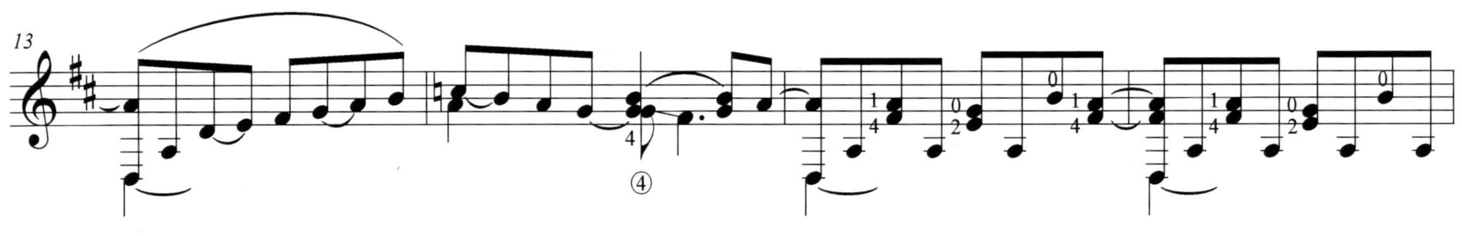

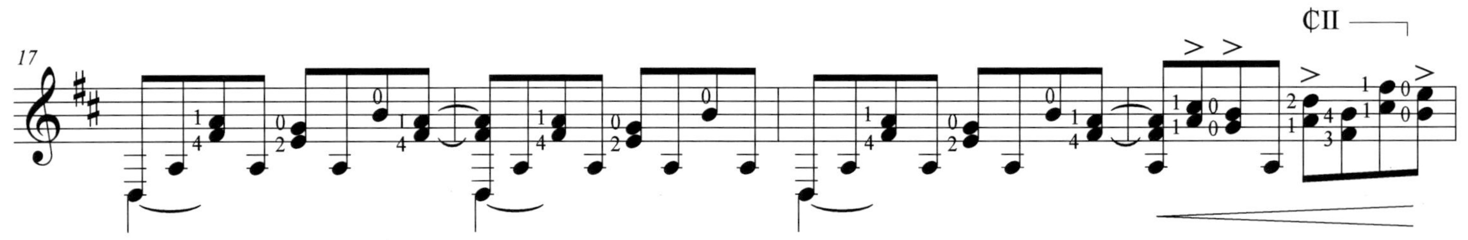

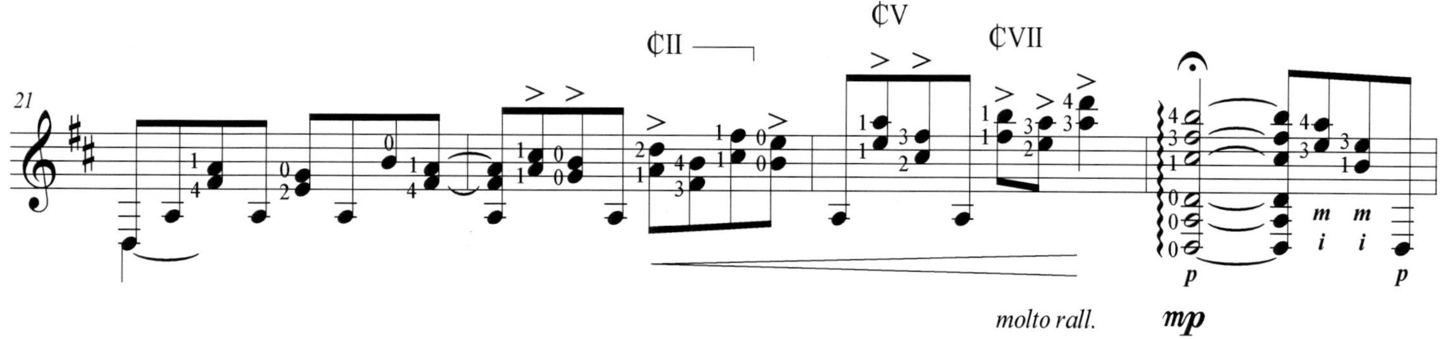
21
CII
CV
CVII
molto rall.
mp

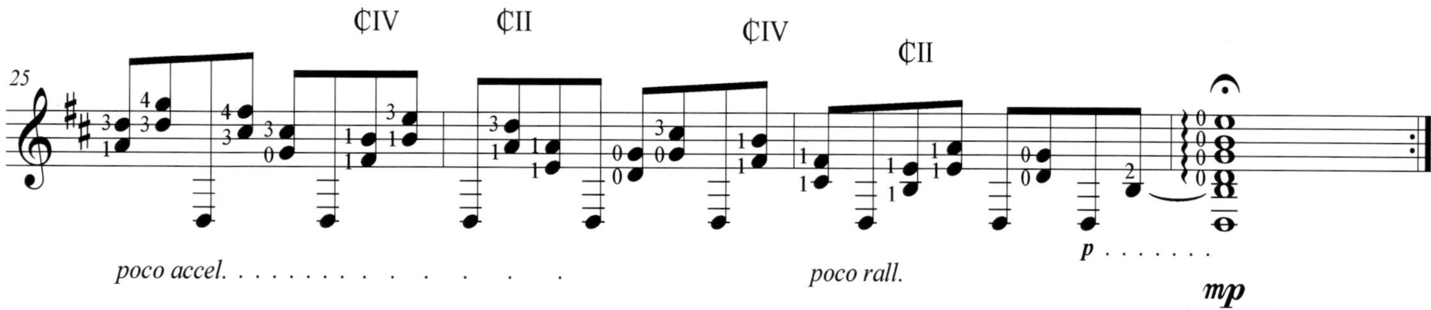
25
CIV
CII
CIV
CII
poco accel. . . . .
poco rall.
p . . . .
mp

a tempo
29

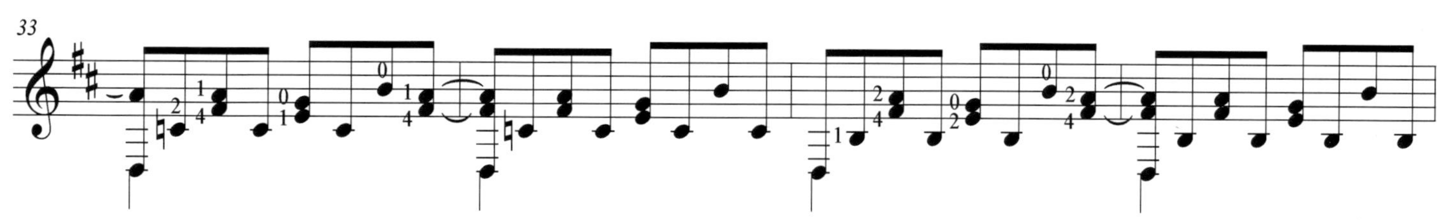
33

rallentando
37

a tempo
41
CII

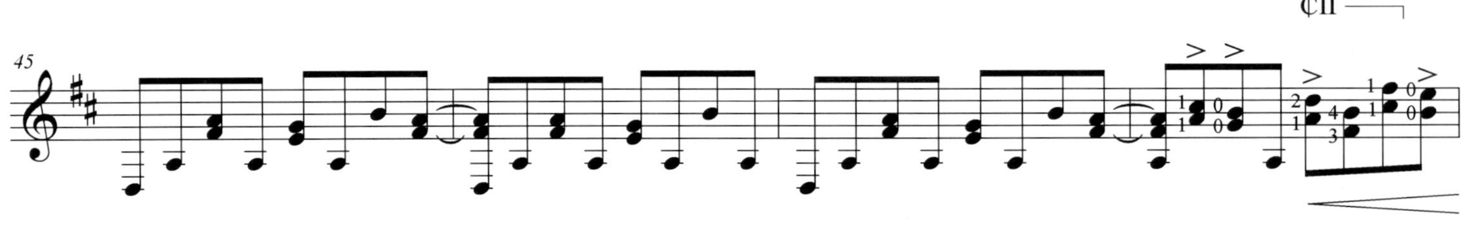
45
CII

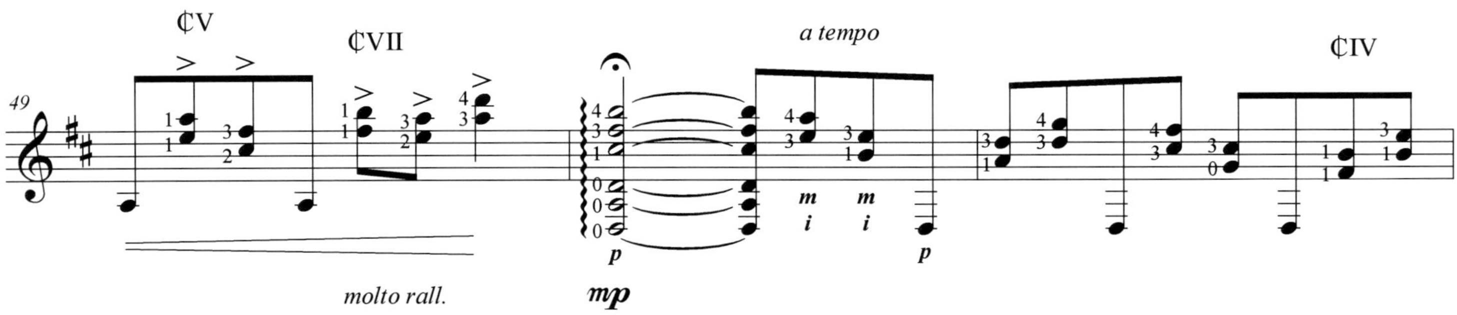
CV
CVII
a tempo
CIV
49
molto rall.
mp

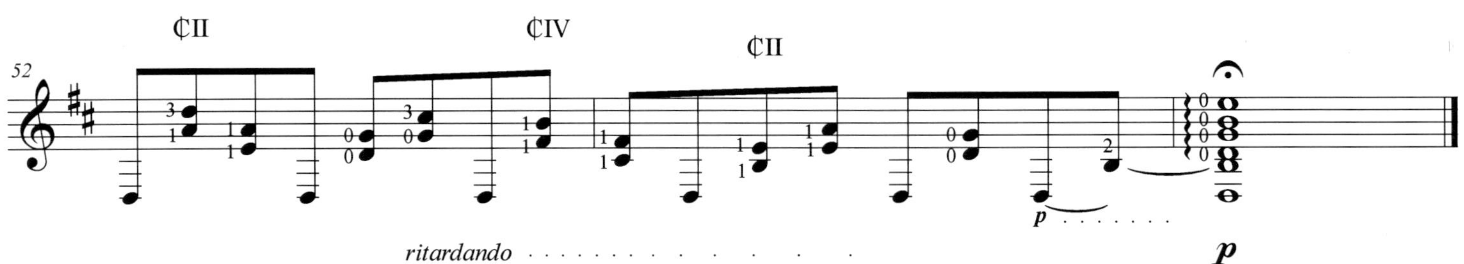
CII
CIV
CII
52
ritardando
p

El Gato

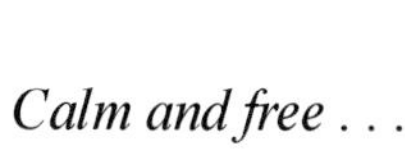

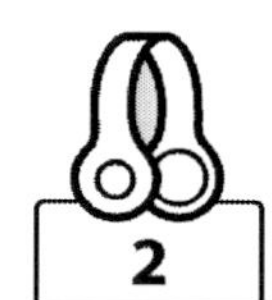

Larry Hammett

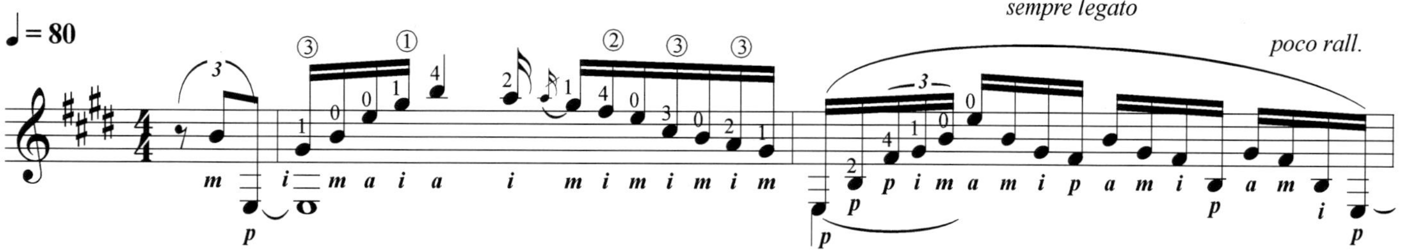

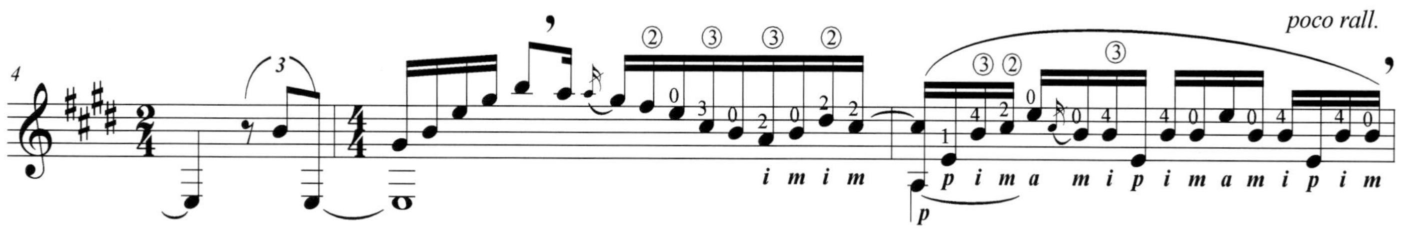

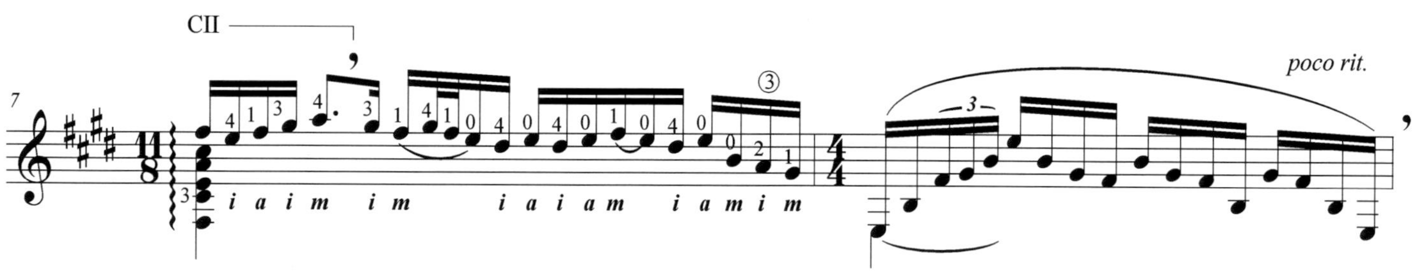

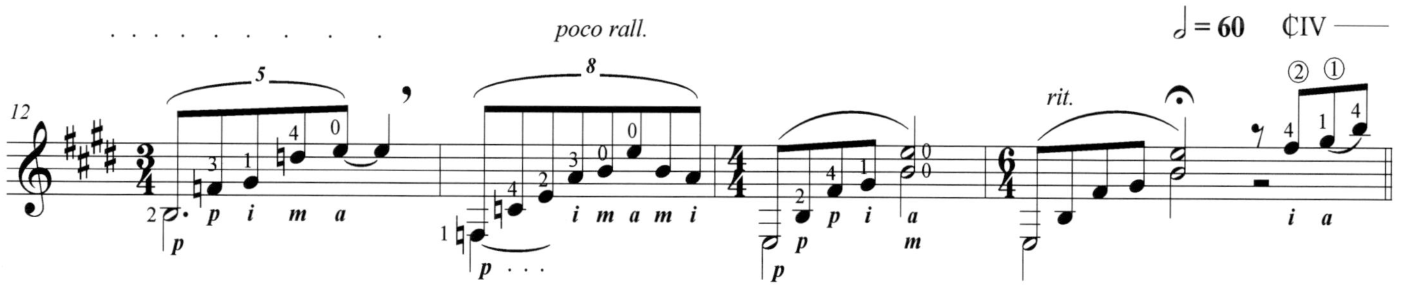

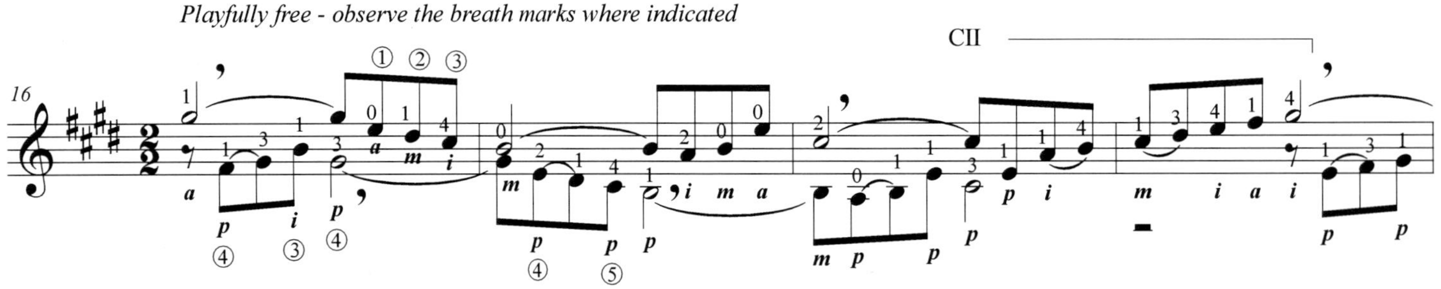
Playfully free - observe the breath marks where indicated
CII
16

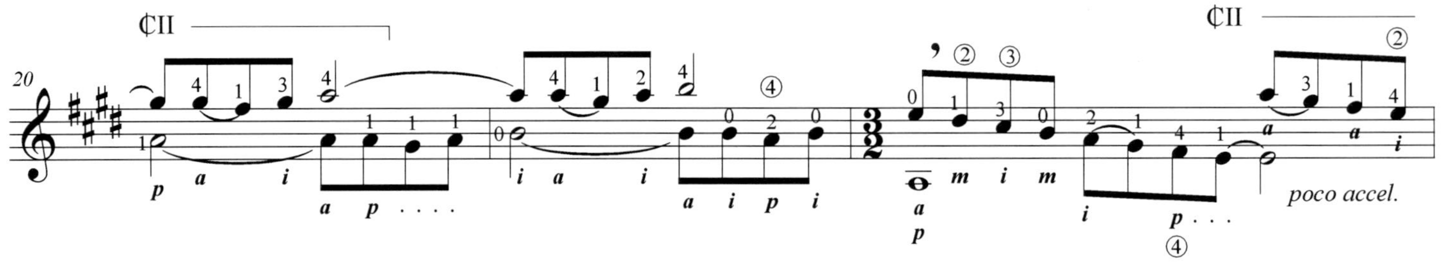
₵II
₵II
20
poco accel.

a piacere . . . .
₵II
poco rall.
23

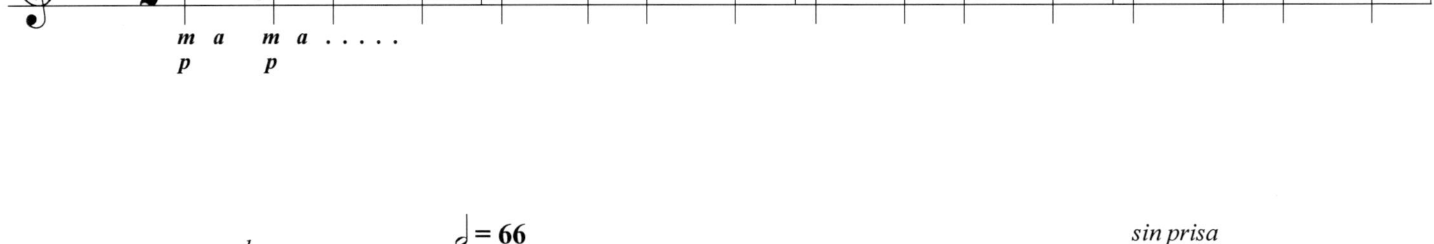
poco accel.
𝅗𝅥 = 66
sin prisa
27

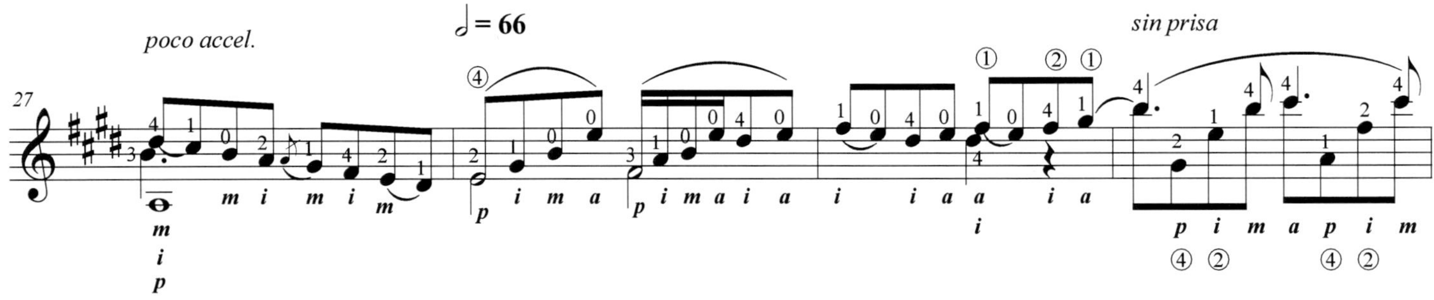
31

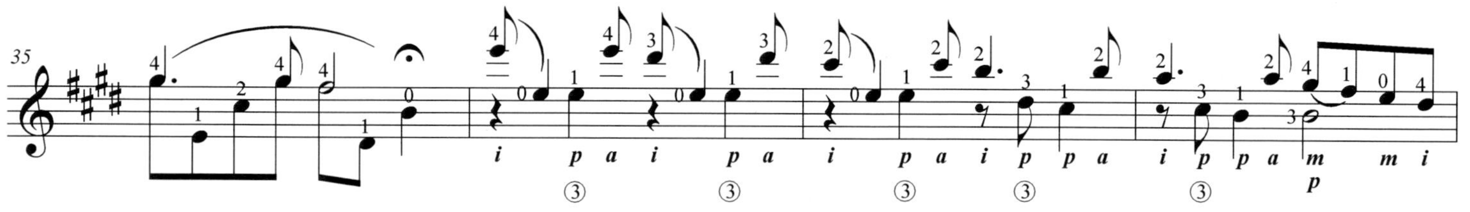
35
i p a i p a i p a i p p a i p p a m p m i
③ ③ ③ ③ ③

rallentando
39
a p m i i m i p p i m a m i p p . . . . i m a m i

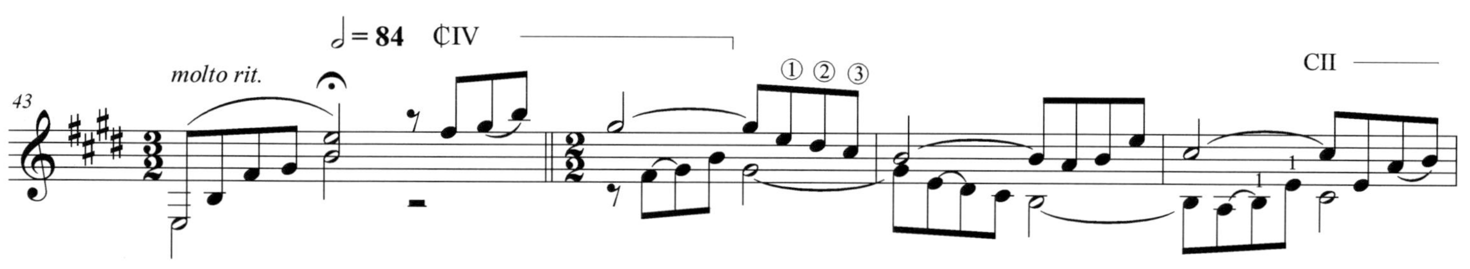
steady tempo . . . .
𝅗𝅥 = 84 ₵IV
molto rit.
43
① ② ③
CII

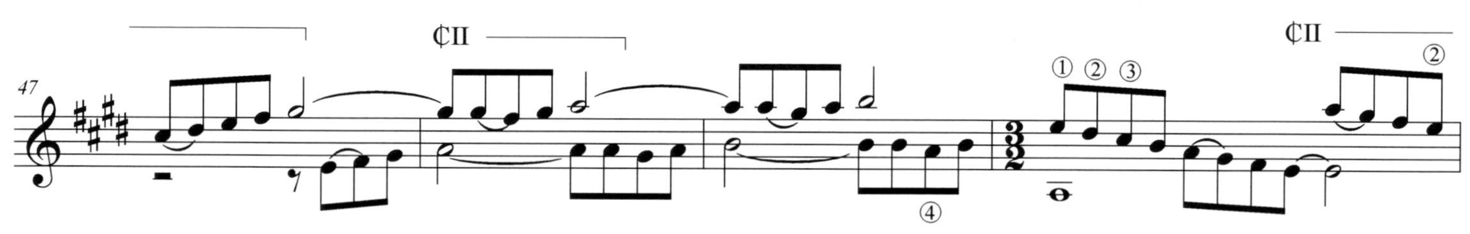
47
₵II
① ② ③
₵II
②
④

₵II
51

55
①
②
①

59
①
②
①

63

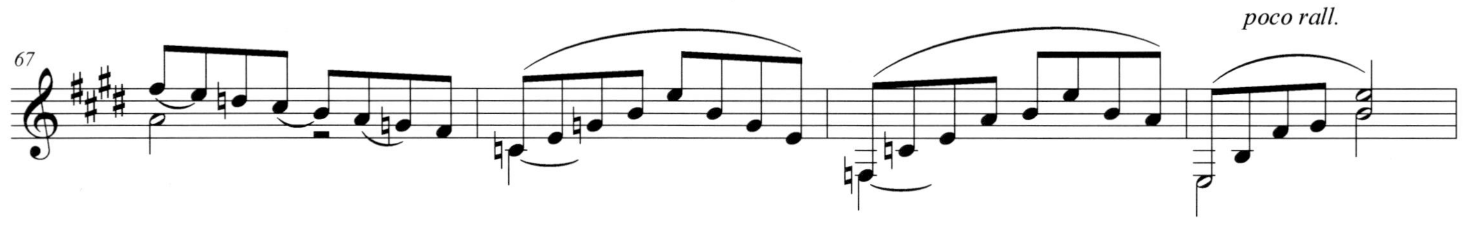
67
poco rall.

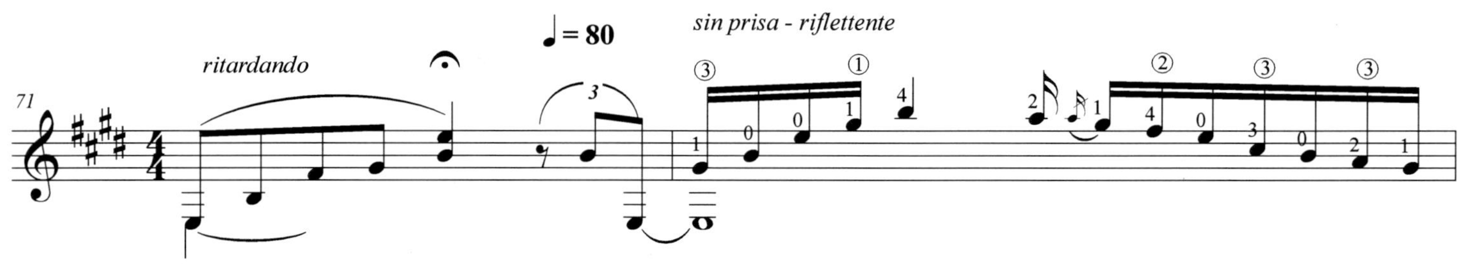
71
ritardando
♩= 80
sin prisa - riflettente

poco rit.
poco rall.
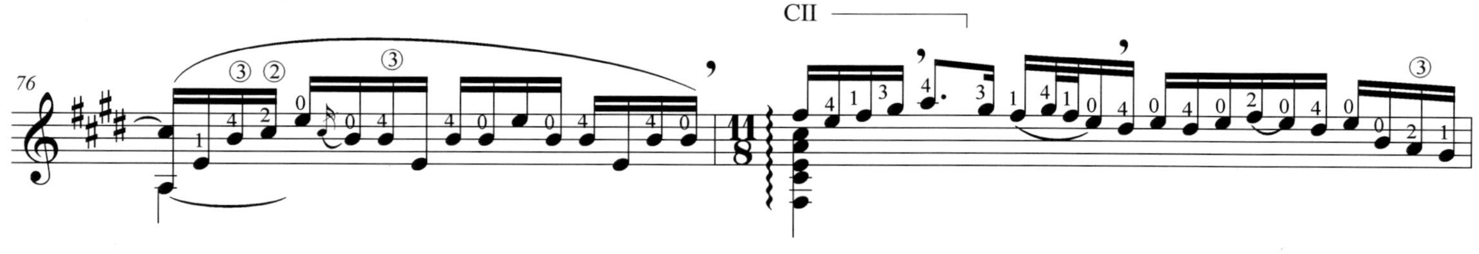
CII
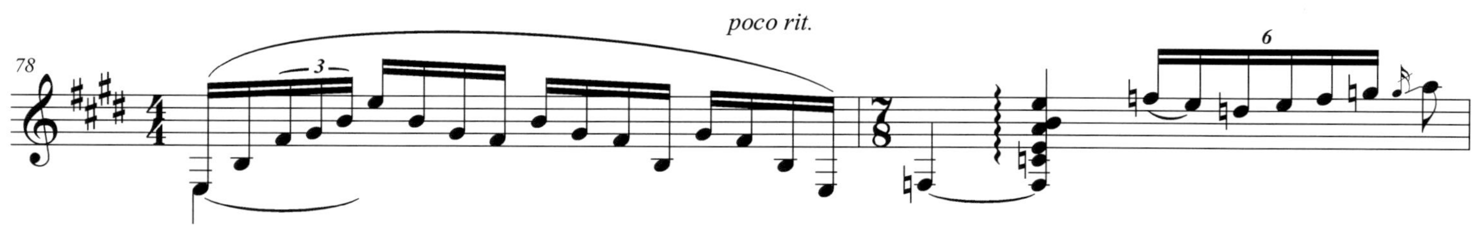
poco rit.
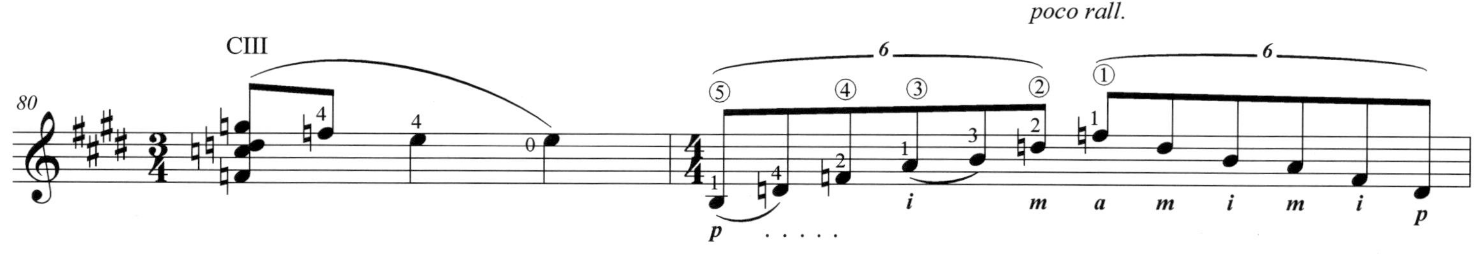
CIII
poco rall.
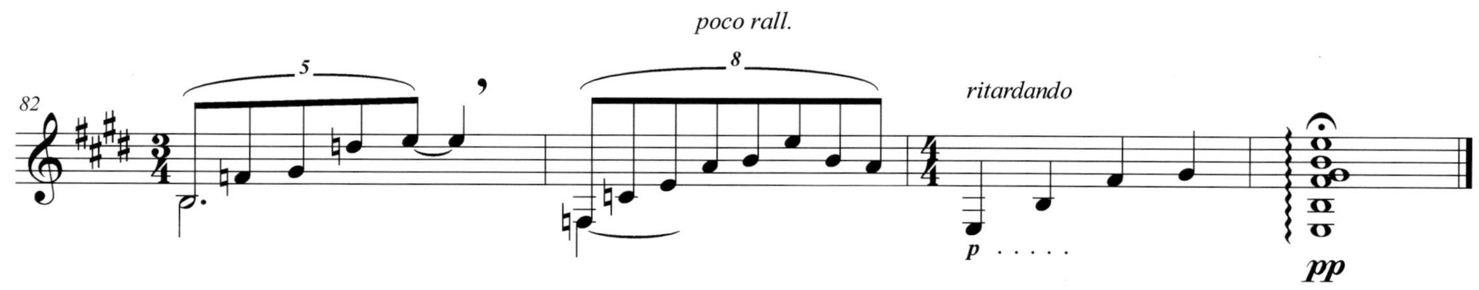
poco rall.
ritardando
pp

Blue Manx

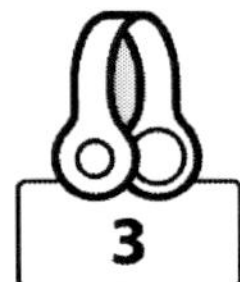

3rd string to F#
6th string to D

Larry Hammett

misterioso - (poco rubato) - (see performance notes)

Circa ♩ = 72

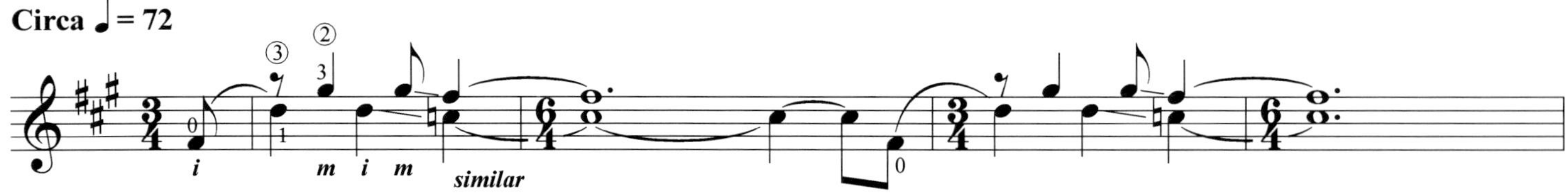

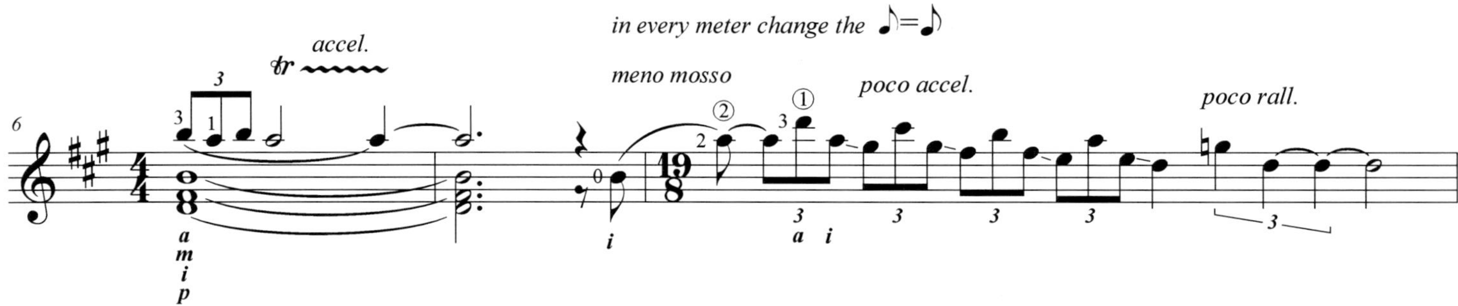

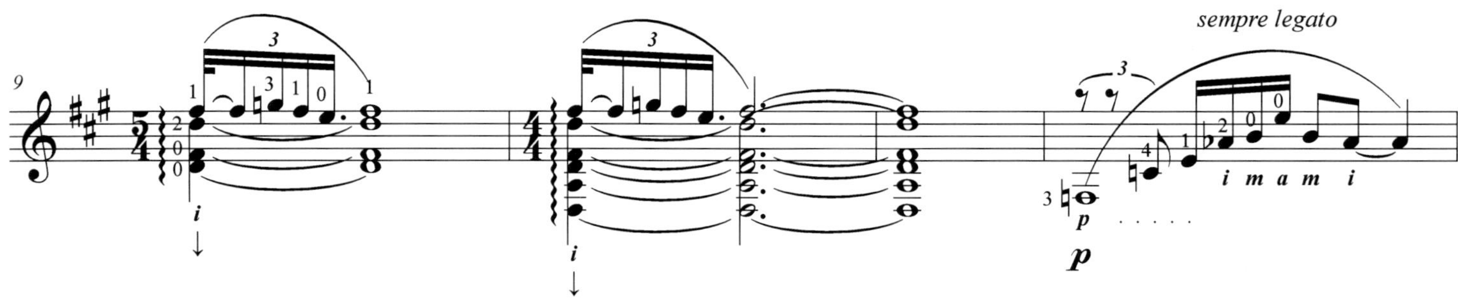

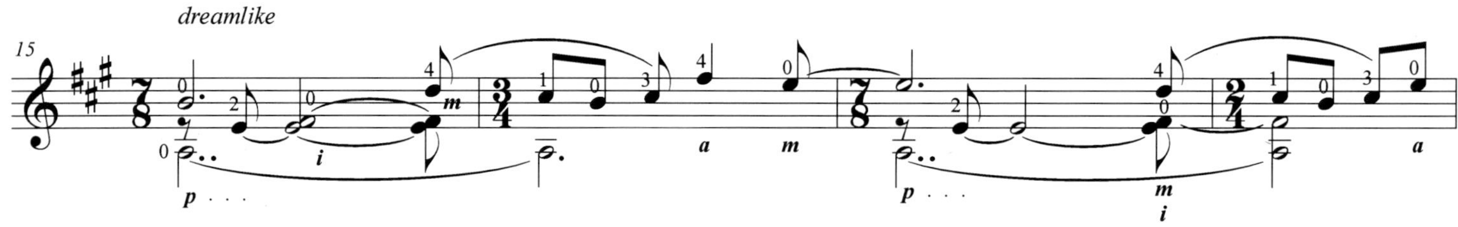

poco ritardando
♩= 88 tranquillo a tempo
sempre legato
poco ritardando
poco accel.
rall.

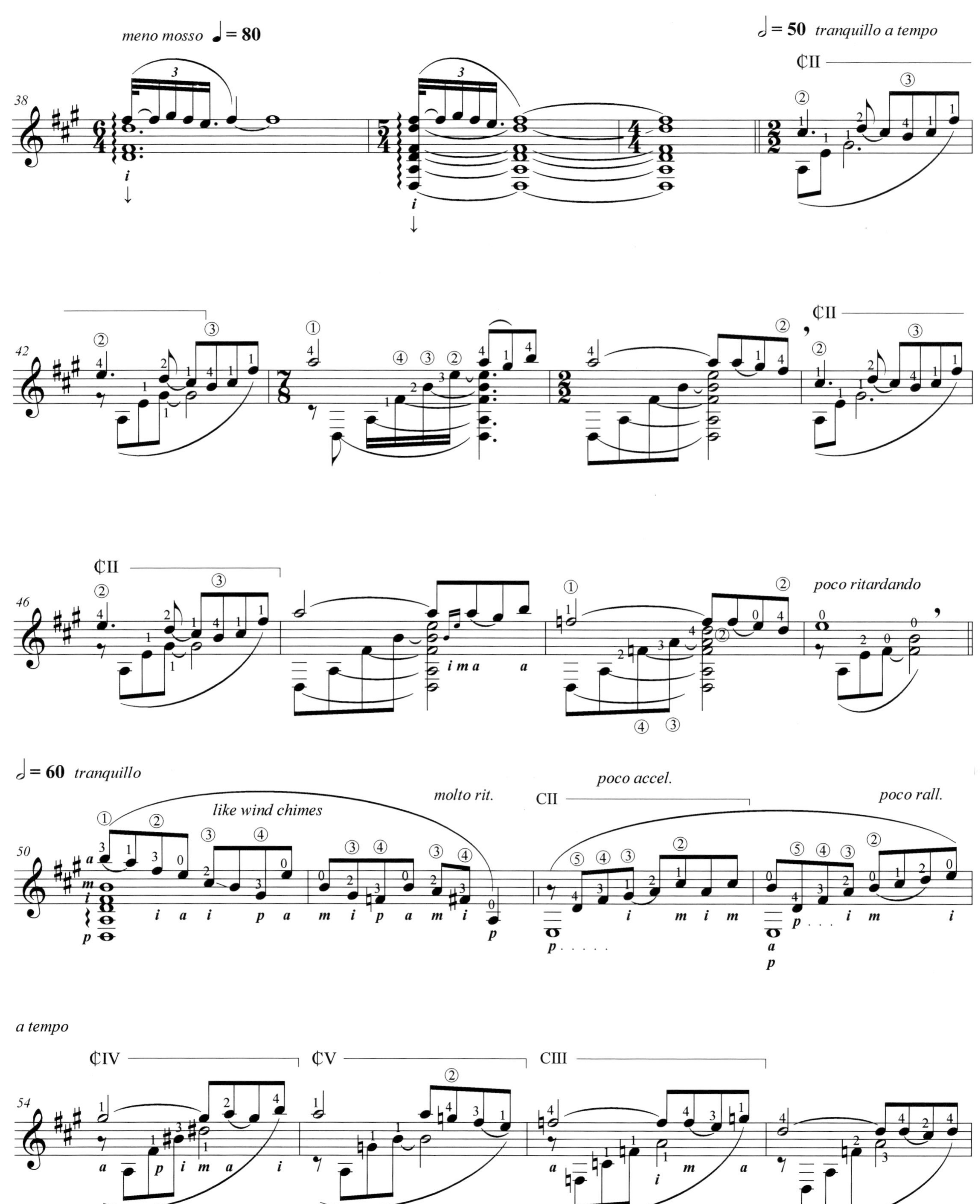

meno mosso ♩= 80
𝅗𝅥 = 50 tranquillo a tempo
poco ritardando
𝅗𝅥 = 60 tranquillo
like wind chimes
molto rit.
poco accel.
poco rall.
a tempo

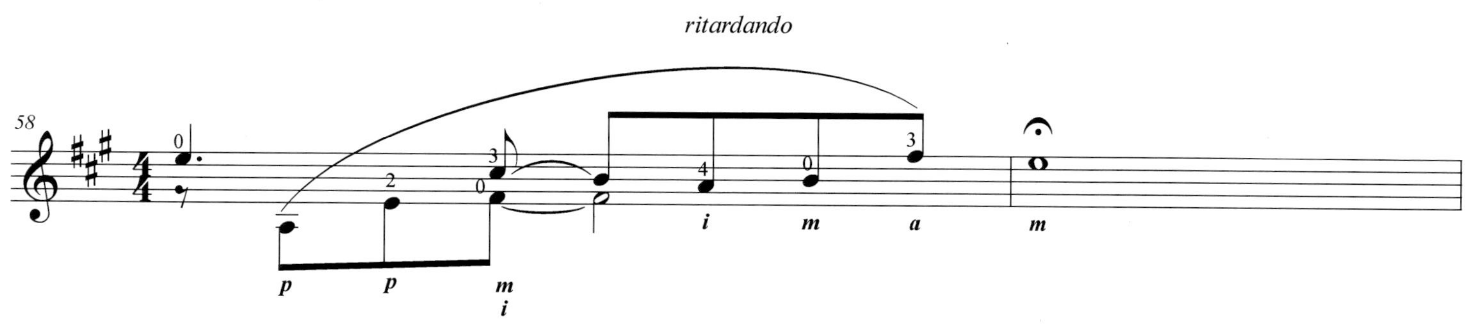
ritardando
58
p p m i
i m a m

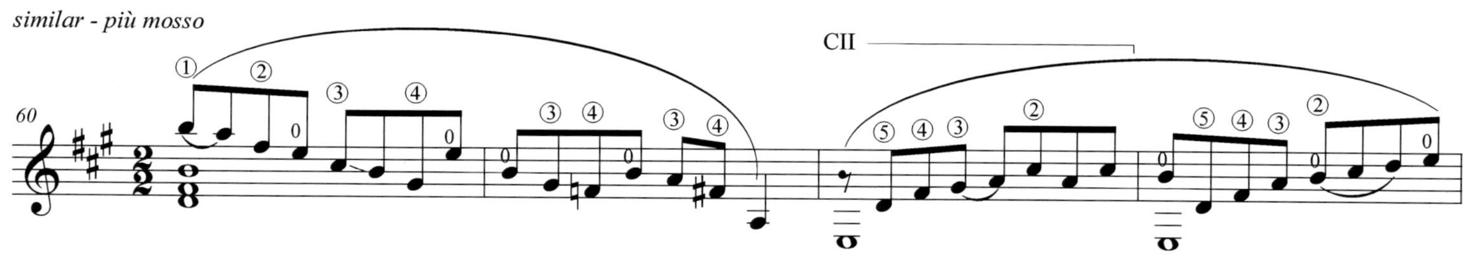
similar - più mosso
60
CII

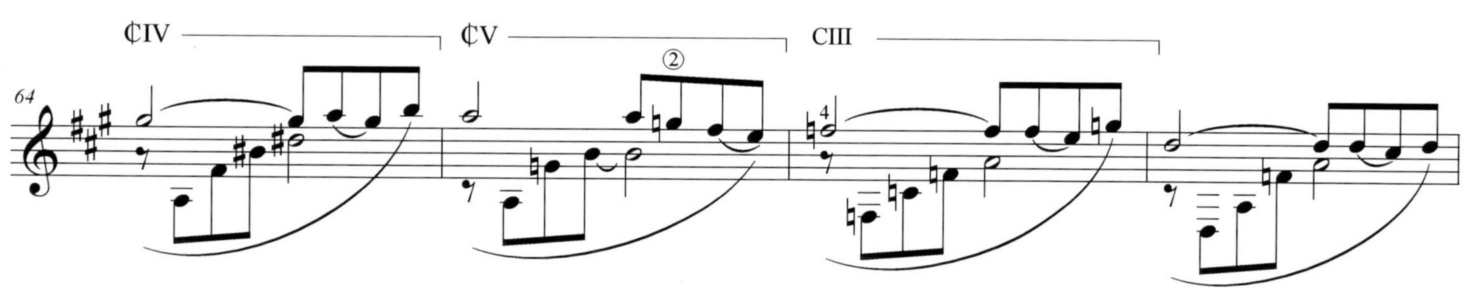
64
¢IV
¢V
CIII

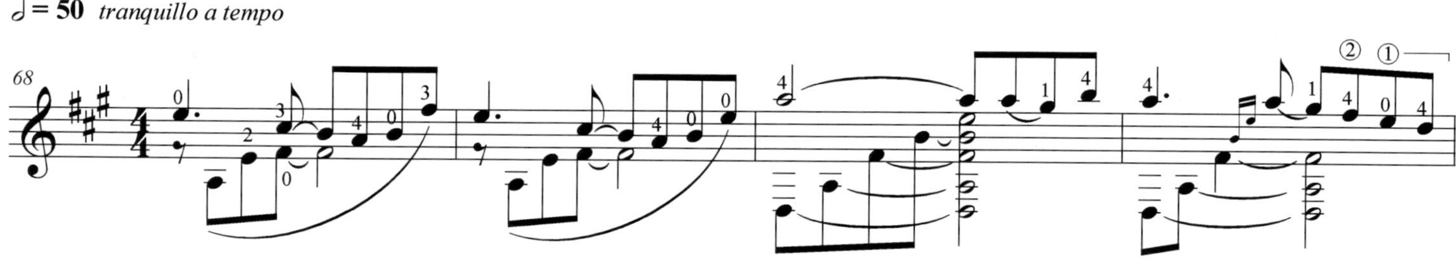
𝅗𝅥 = 50 tranquillo a tempo
68

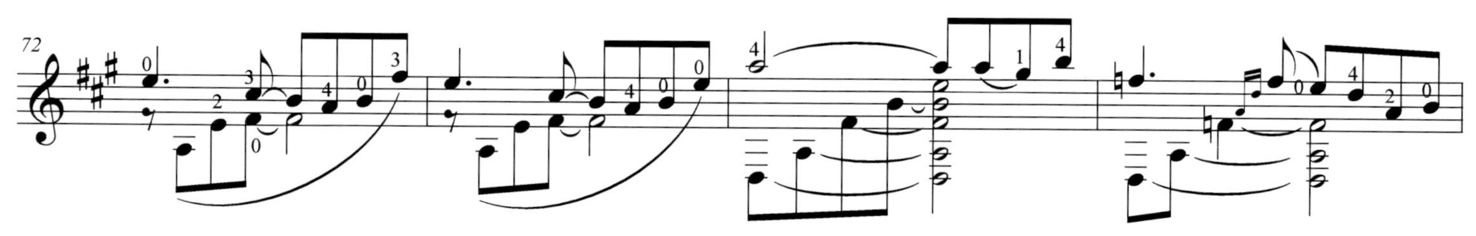
72

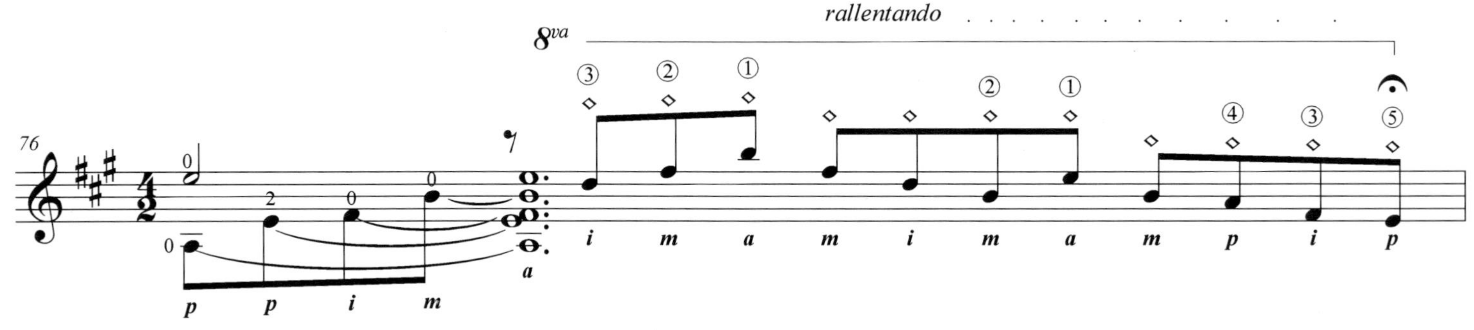
rallentando
8va
76

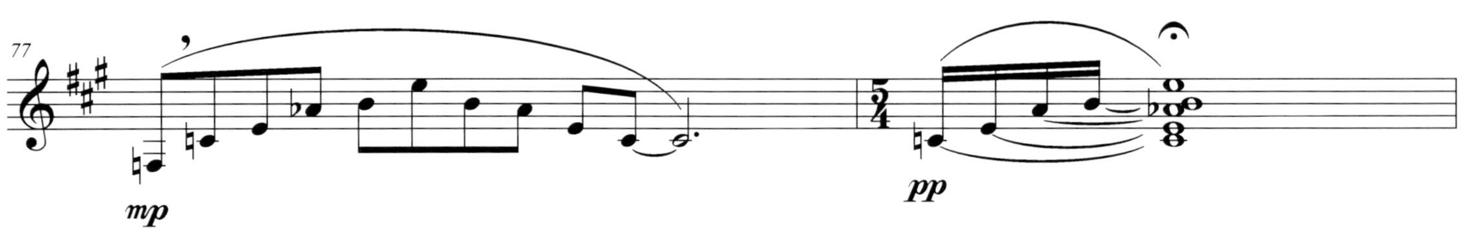
77
mp
pp

riflettente
79

83
mp
mf

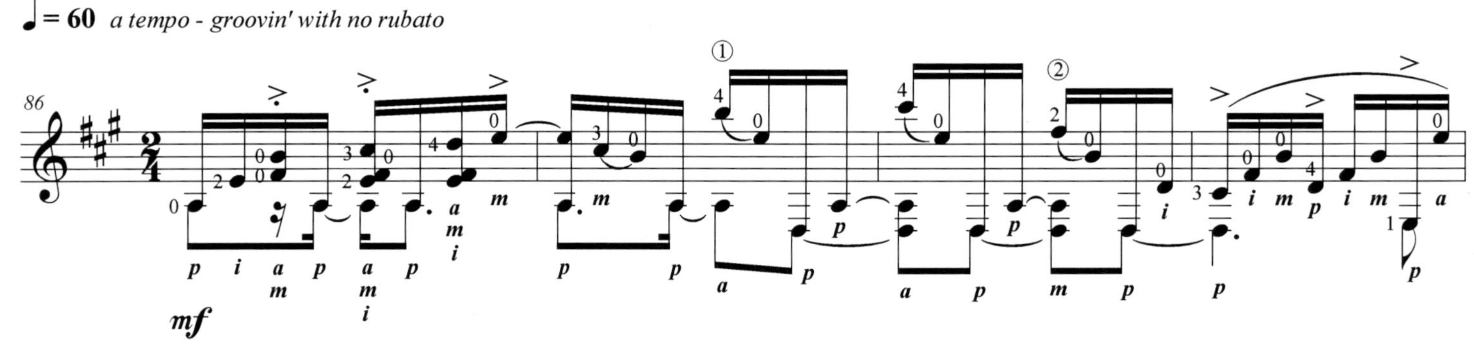
♩= 60 a tempo - groovin' with no rubato
86
mf

8va
molto rit.

Las Gatitas

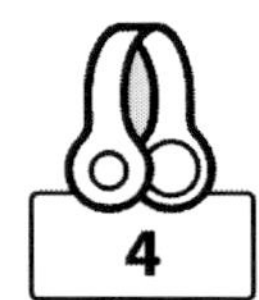

Capo II

Larry Hammett

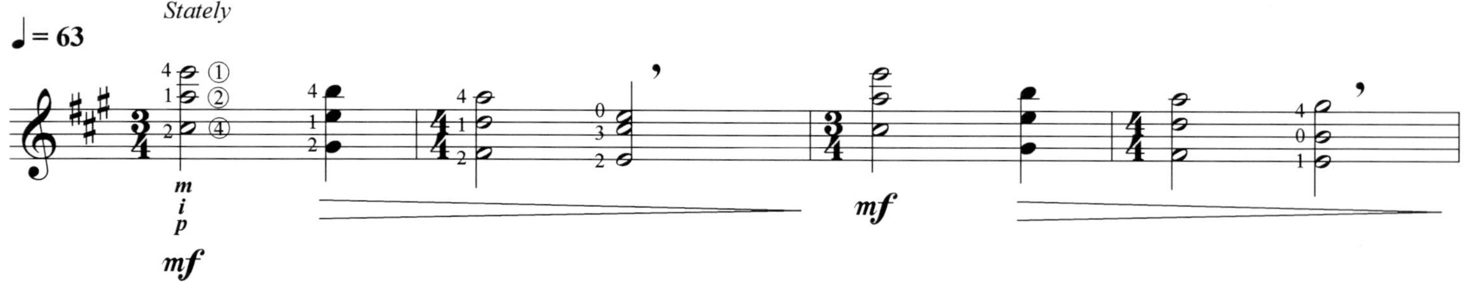

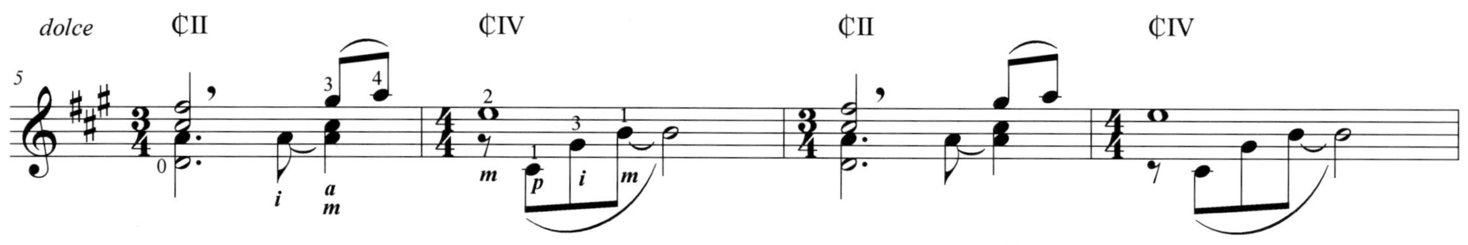

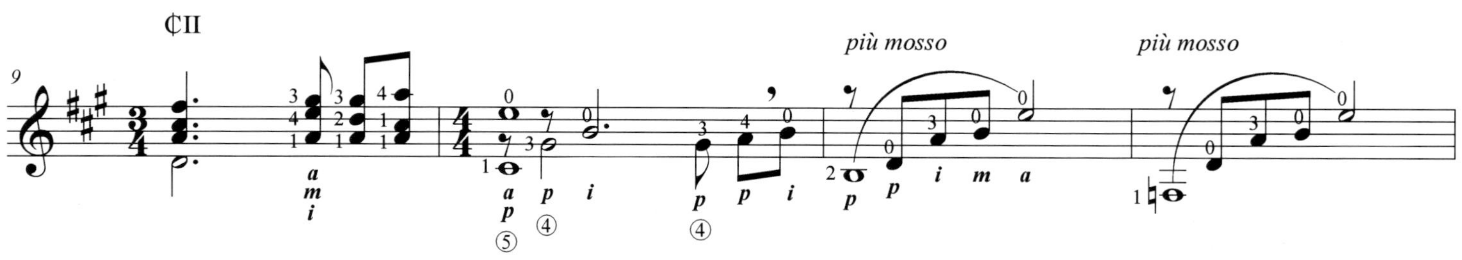

(measure 17 - 34) 1st time rubato with fairly robust tremolo ♩= 92 / 2nd time steady with feathery light tremolo ♩= 151

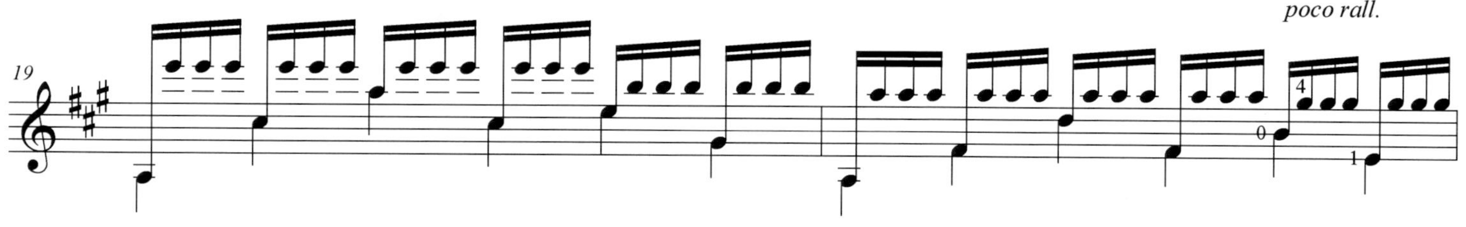
19
poco rall.

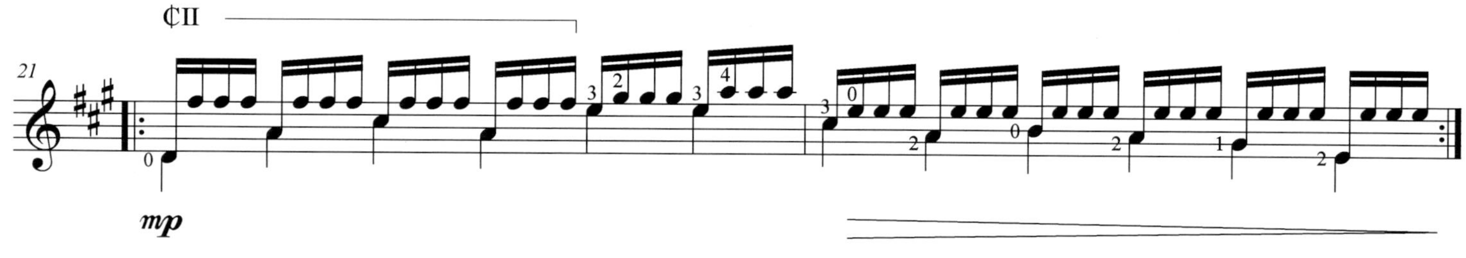
21
CII
mp

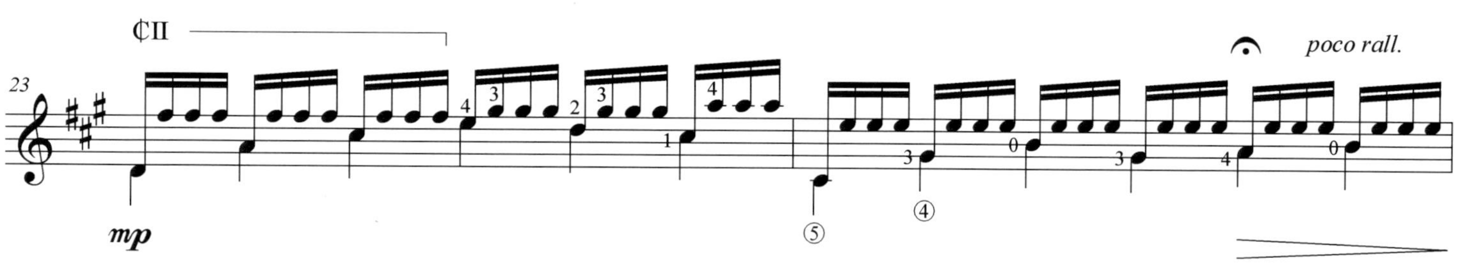
23
CII
poco rall.
mp

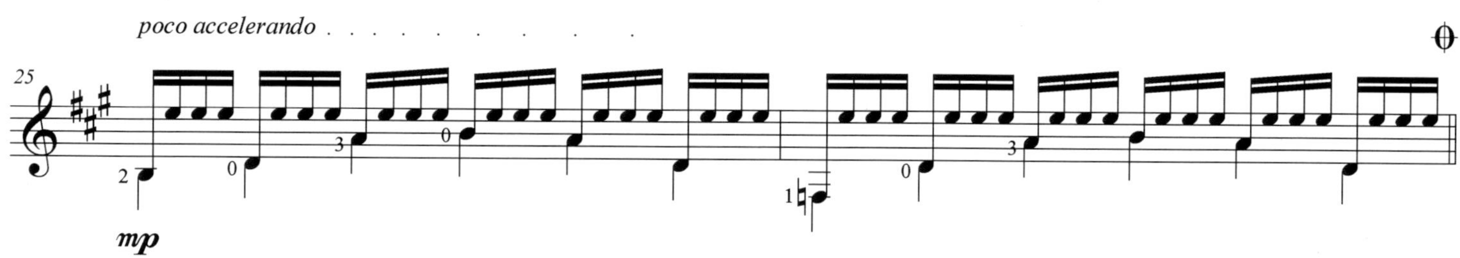
25
poco accelerando
mp

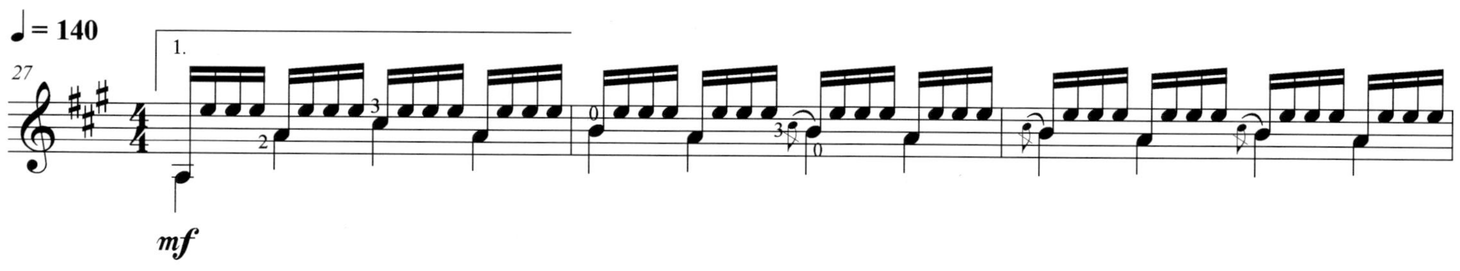
a tempo
♩ = 140
27
1.
mf

30

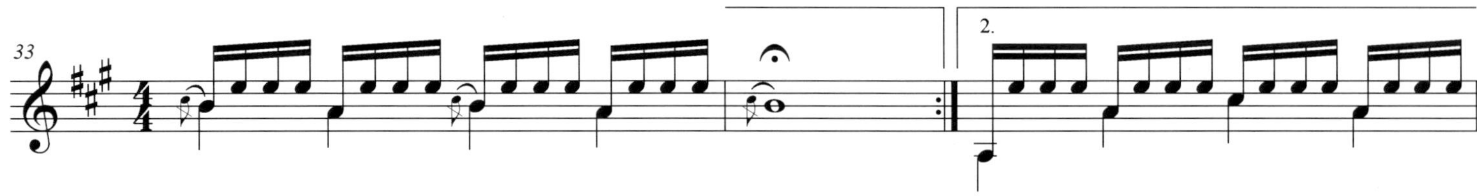
33
2.

36

39

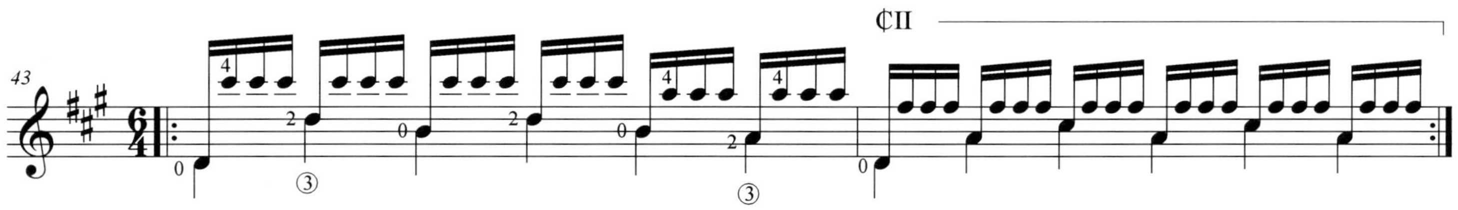
43
CII

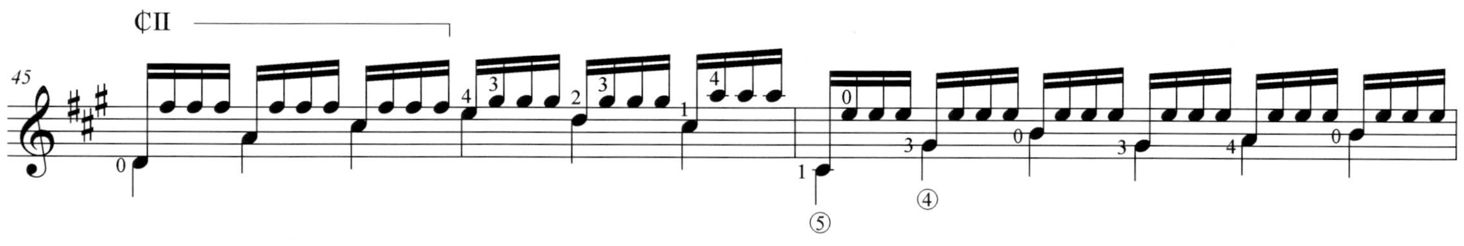

D.S. al Coda

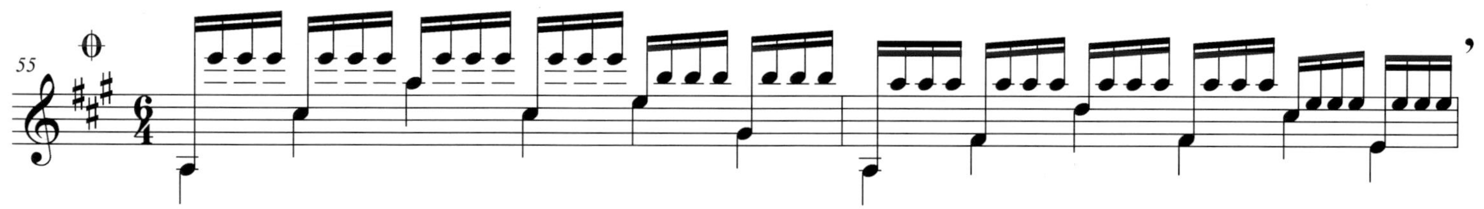

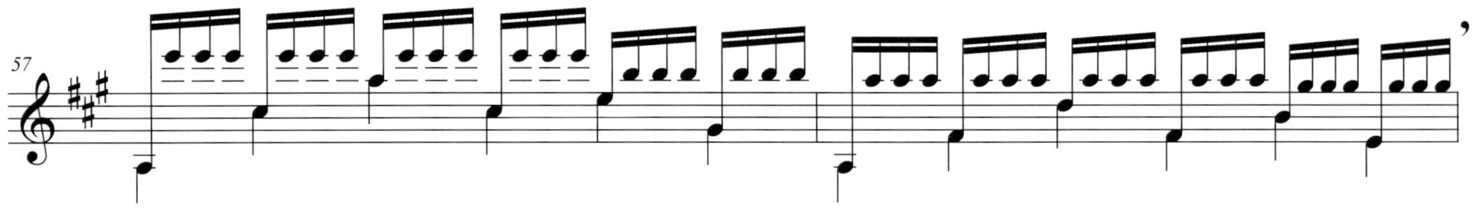
57

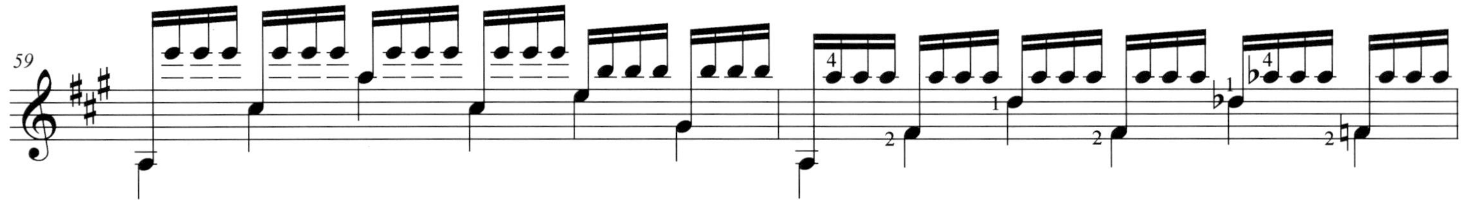
59
4
1
2
2
1
4
2

poco rall.
61
4
1
4
2
2
0
2
4
0
0
0
0

a tempo
63

66

69

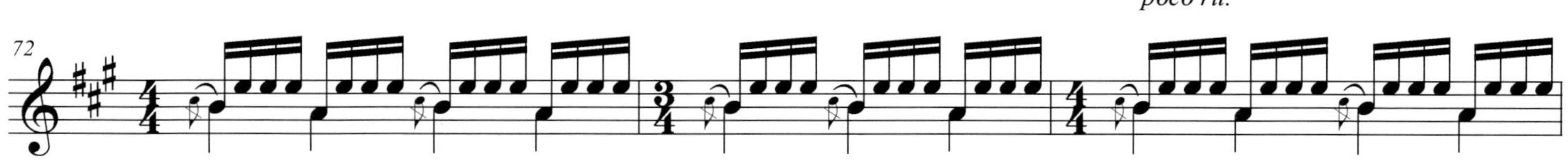
poco rit.
72

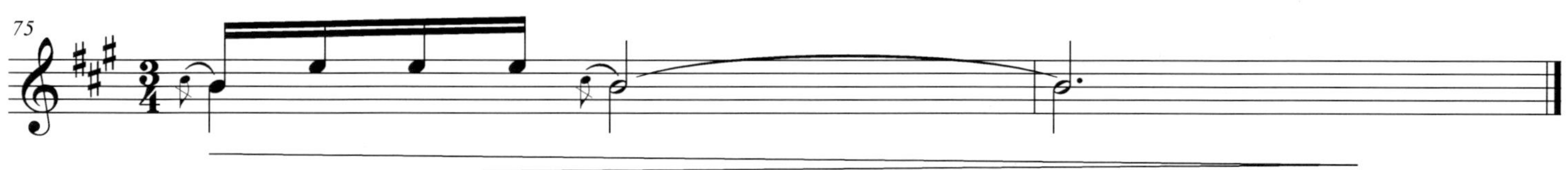
75

Vals de la Gatita

Larry Hammett

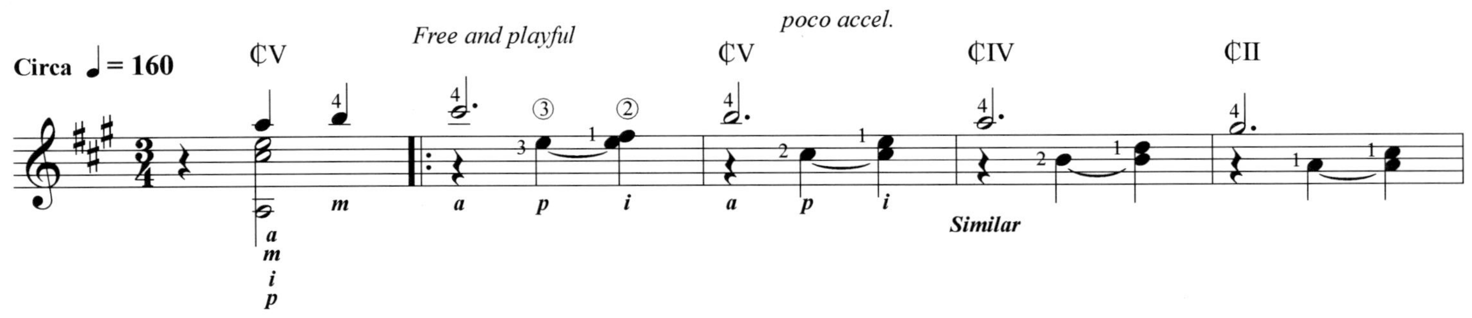

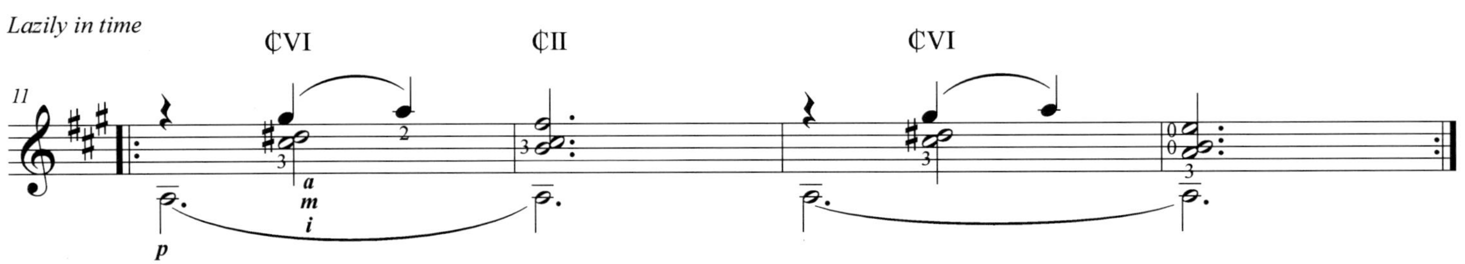

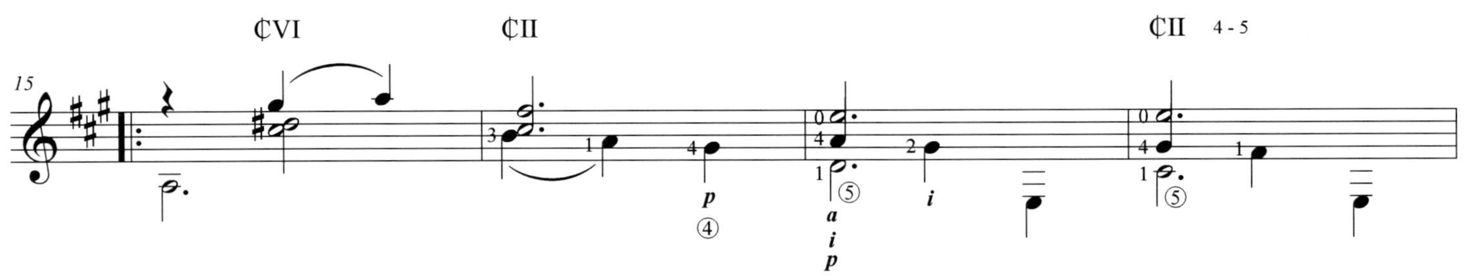

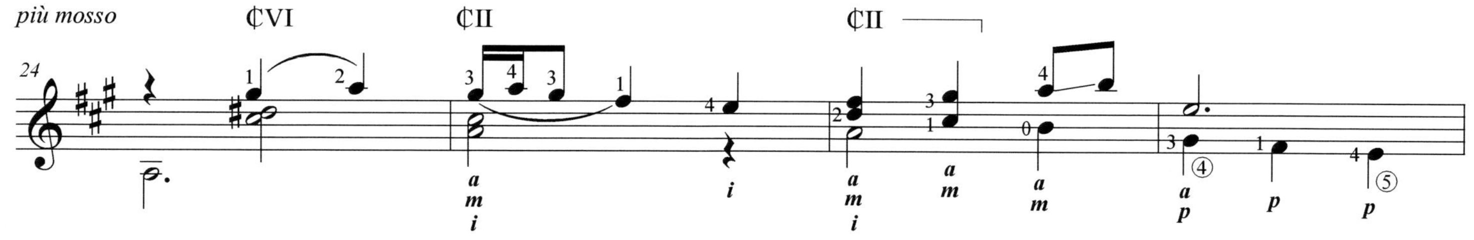
più mosso
₵VI
₵II
₵II
a
m
i
i
a
m
i
a
m
a
m
a
p
p
p

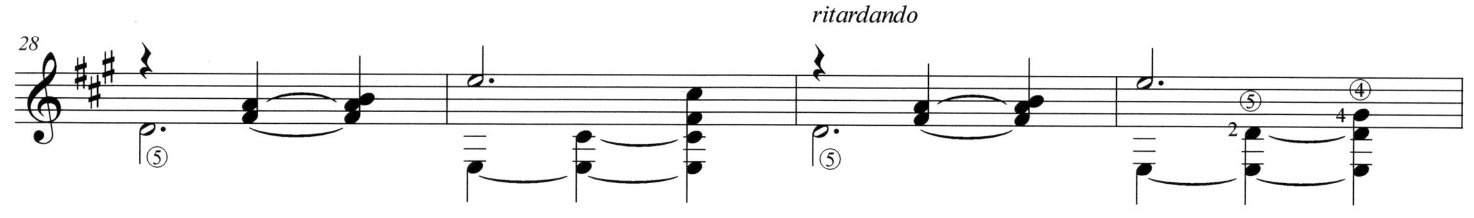
ritardando

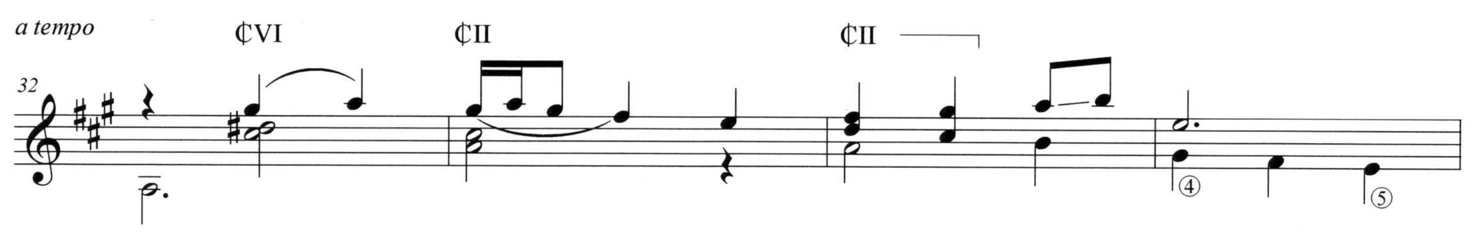
a tempo
₵VI
₵II
₵II

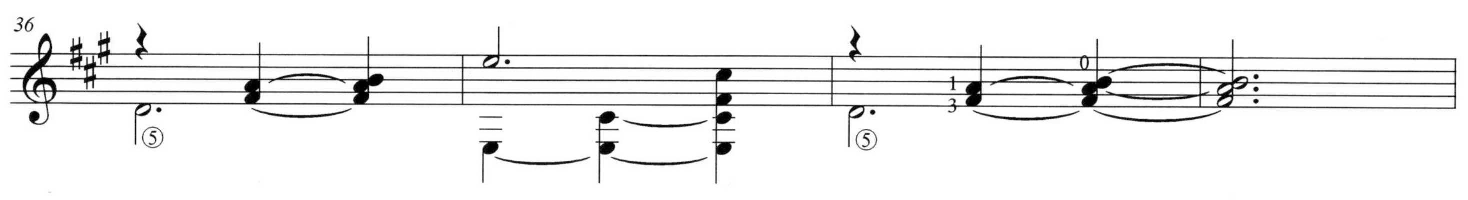

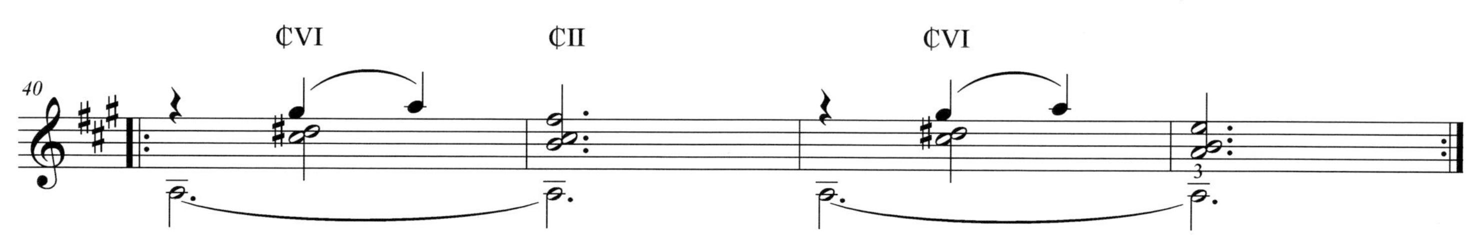
₵VI
₵II
₵VI

poco accel.
44

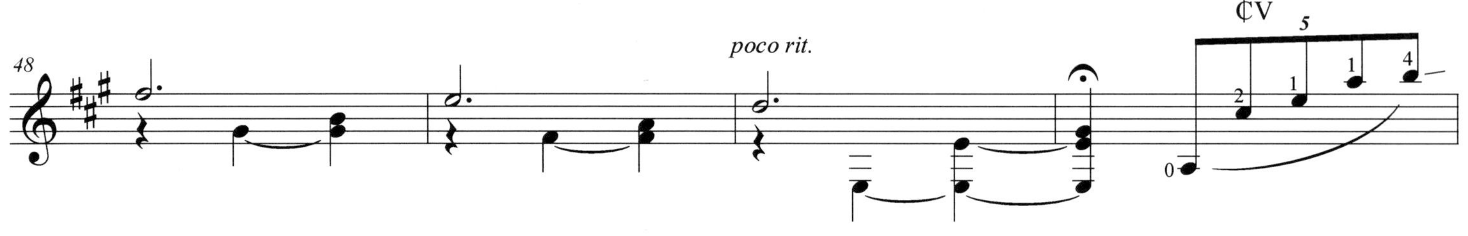
48
poco rit.
₵V

52

ritardando
56

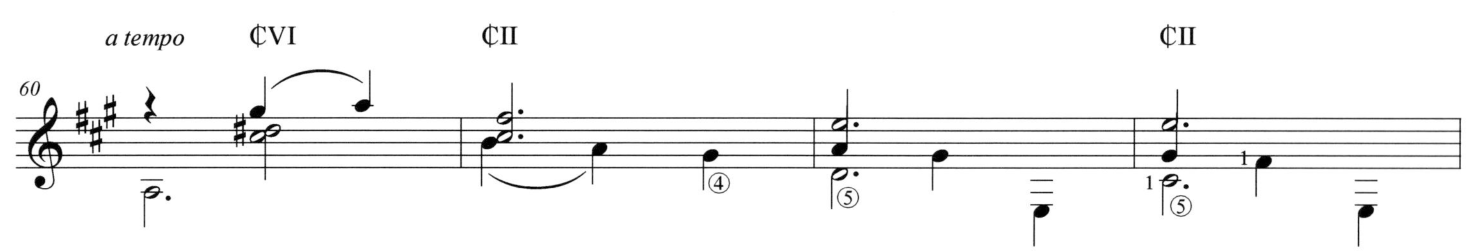
a tempo
₵VI
₵II
₵II
60

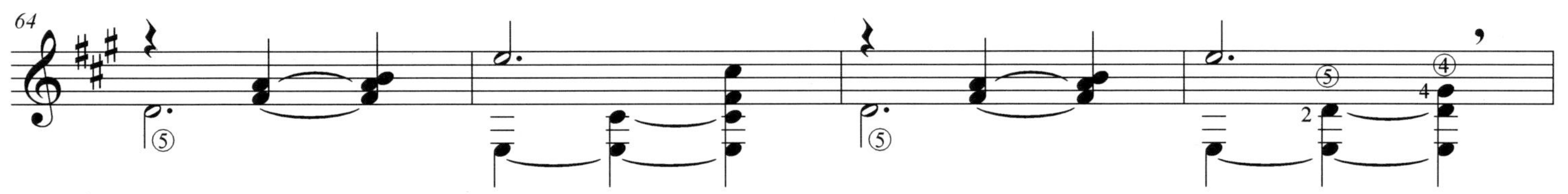
64

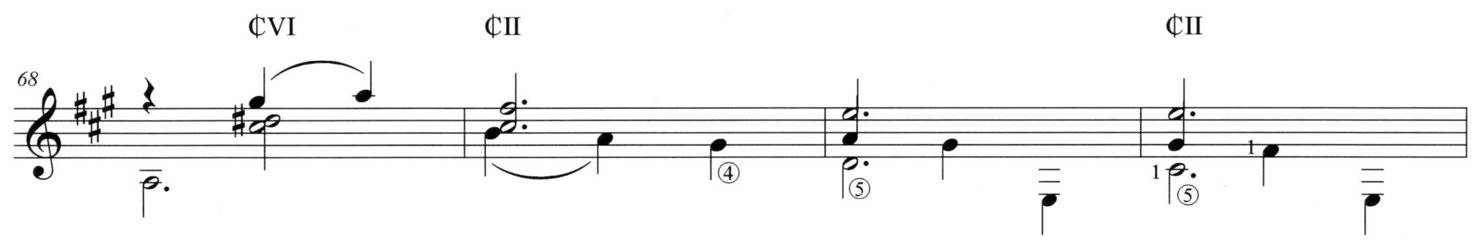
₵VI
₵II
₵II
68

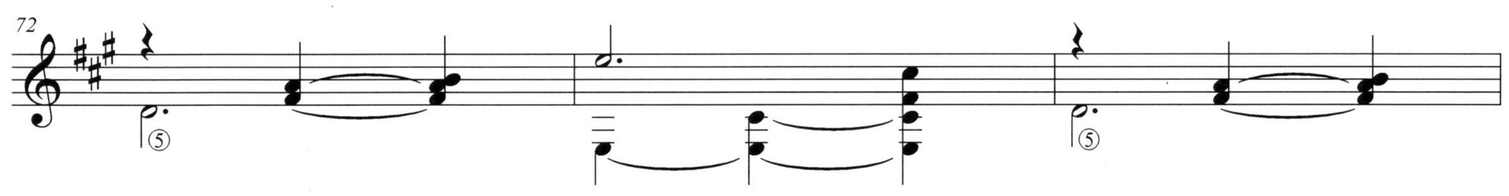
72

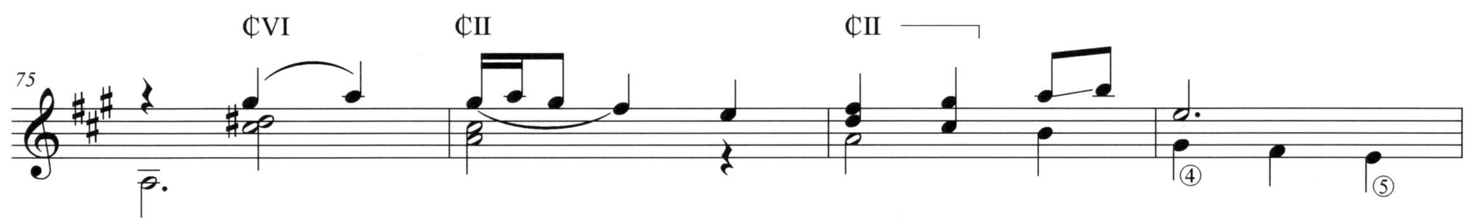
₵VI
₵II
₵II
75

79

83
₵VI
₵II
₵II
④
⑤

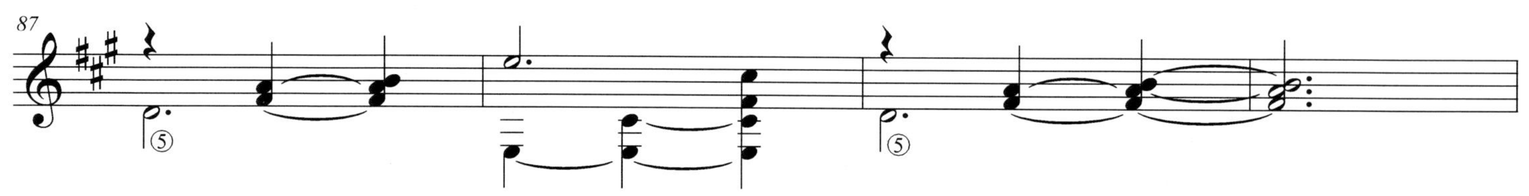
87
⑤
⑤

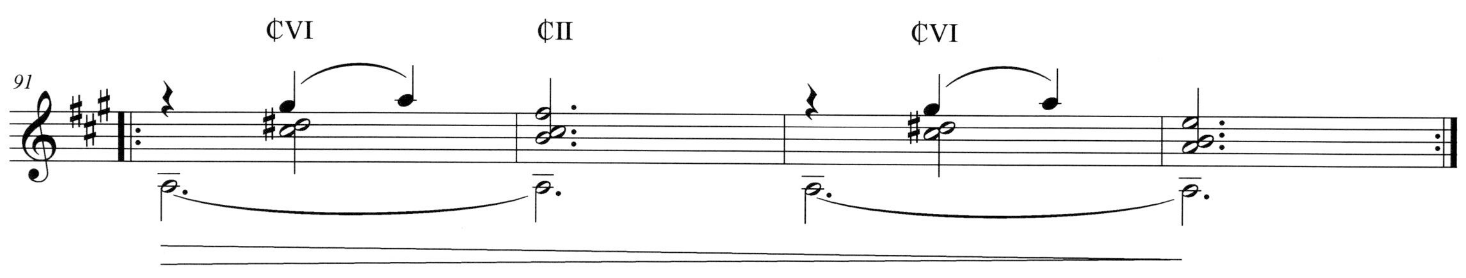
91
₵VI
₵II
₵VI

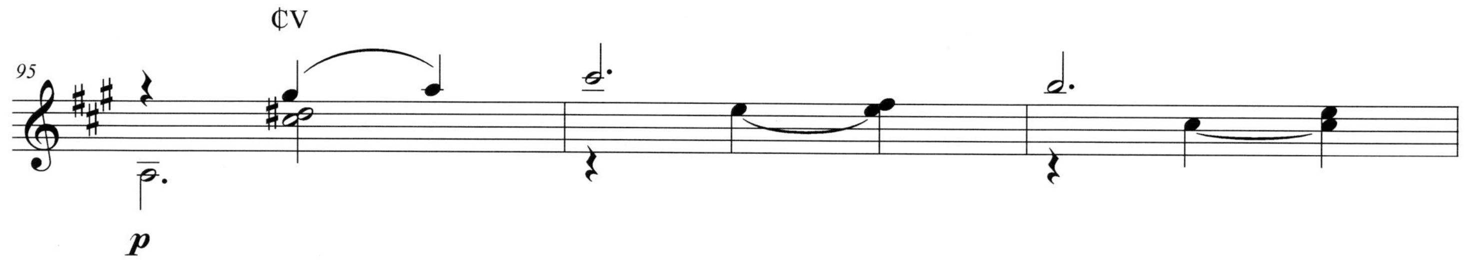
95
₵V
p

98

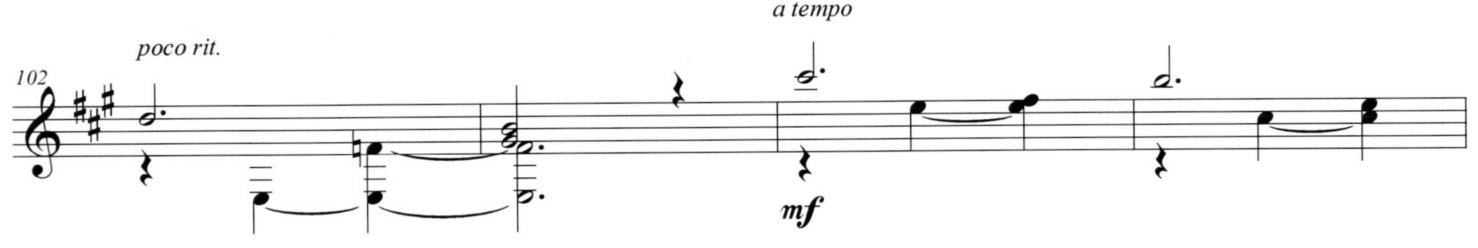
a tempo
poco rit.
102
mf

106

a tempo
ȻVI
ȻII
poco rit.
110

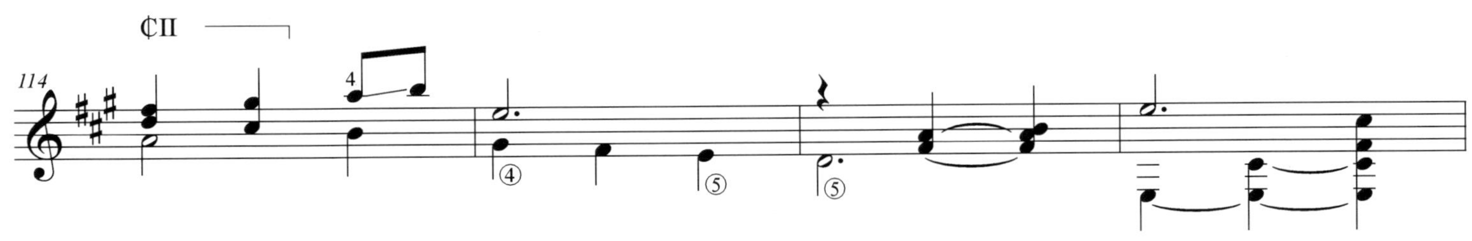
ȻII
114

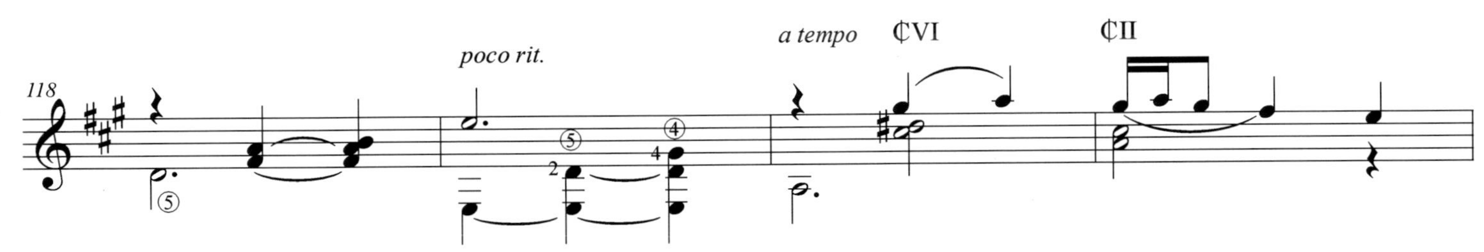
a tempo
ȻVI
ȻII
poco rit.
118

CII
122
⑤

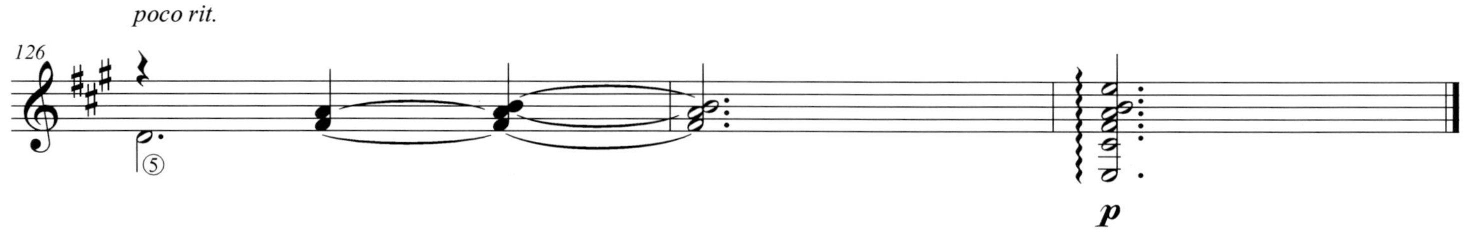
poco rit.
126
⑤
p

El Tigre

Capo III

Larry Hammett

Pensieroso

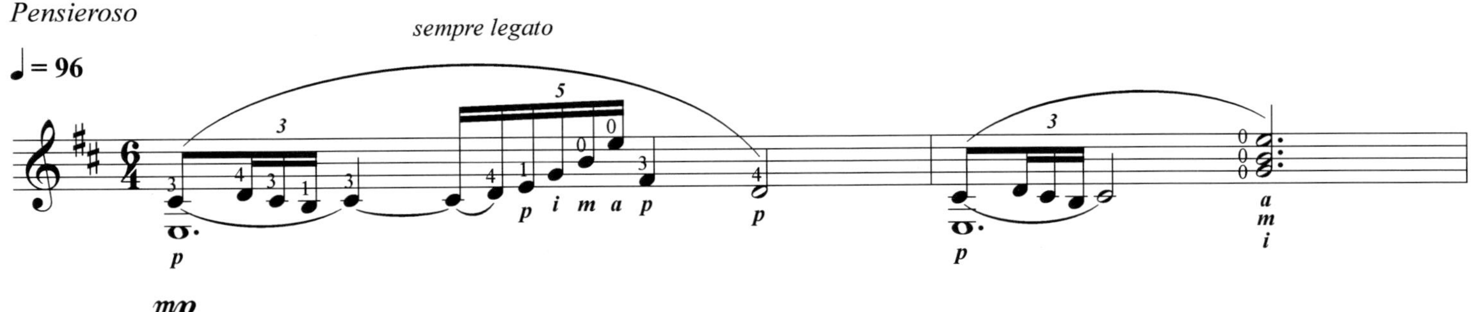

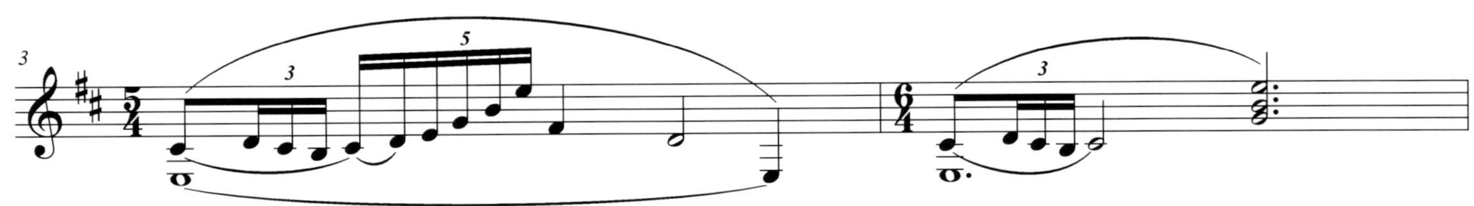

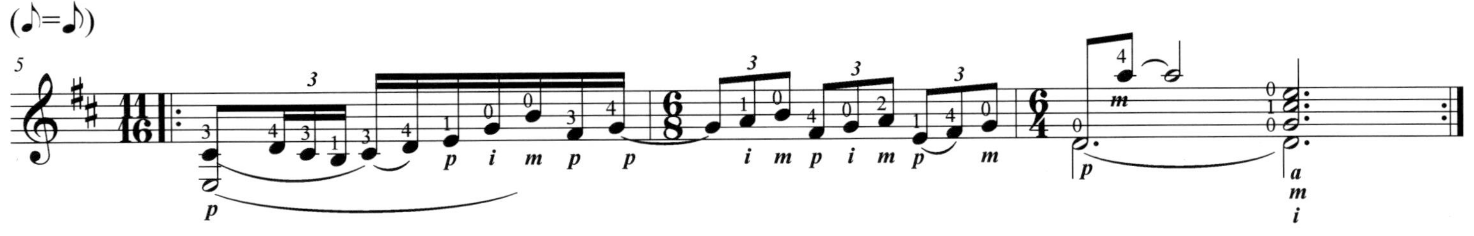

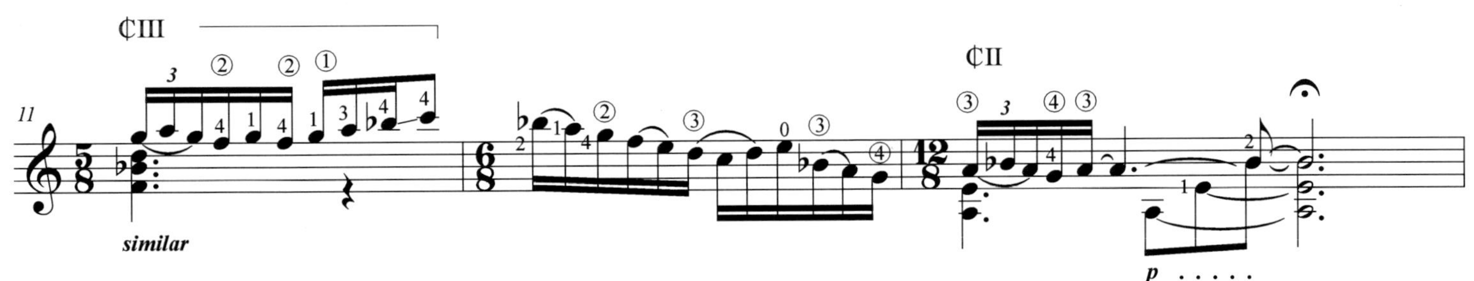

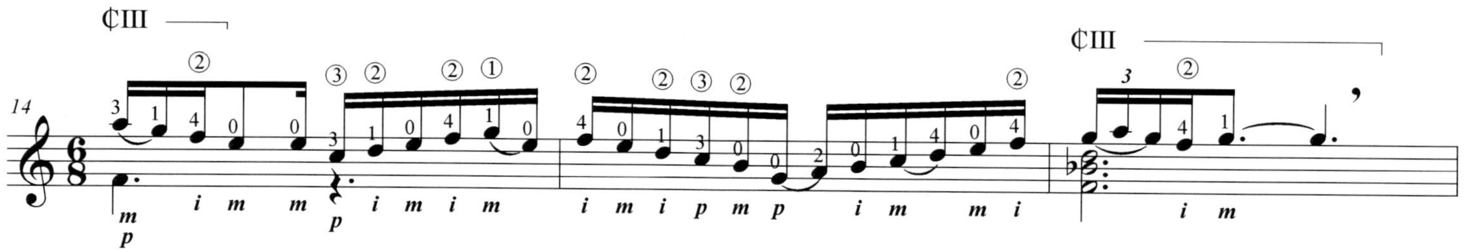
CIII
CIII

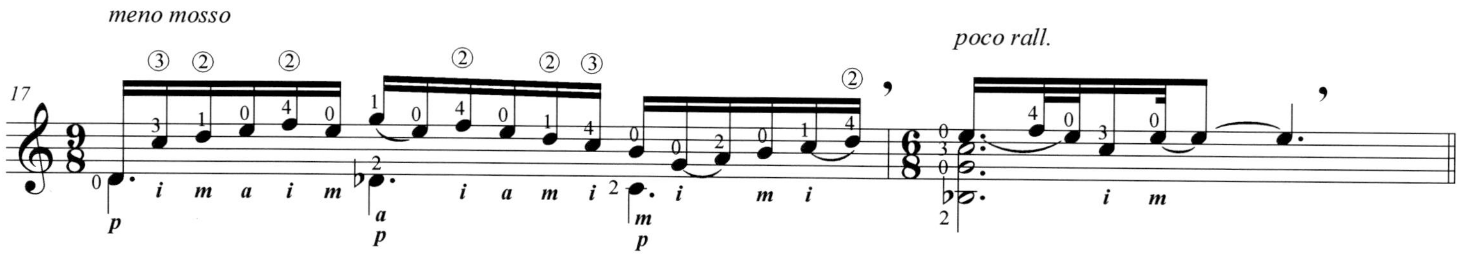
meno mosso
poco rall.

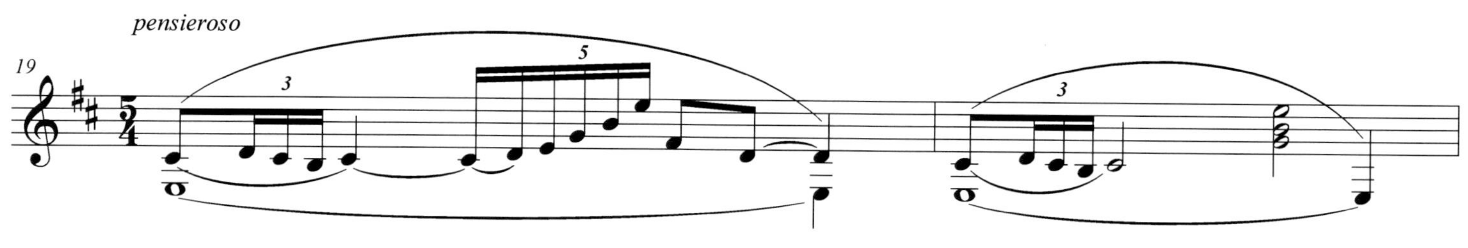
pensieroso

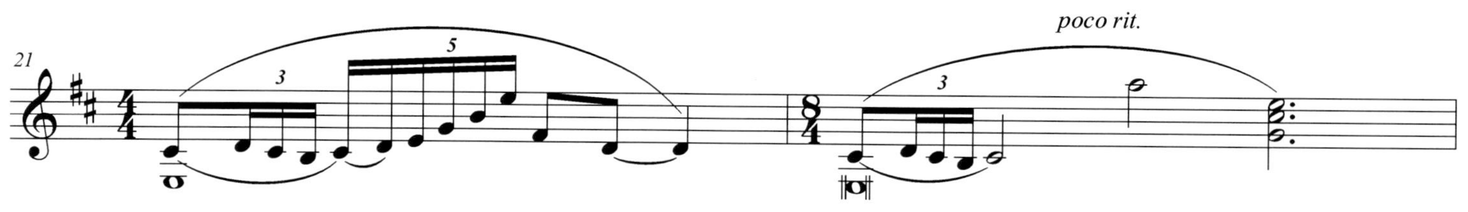
poco rit.

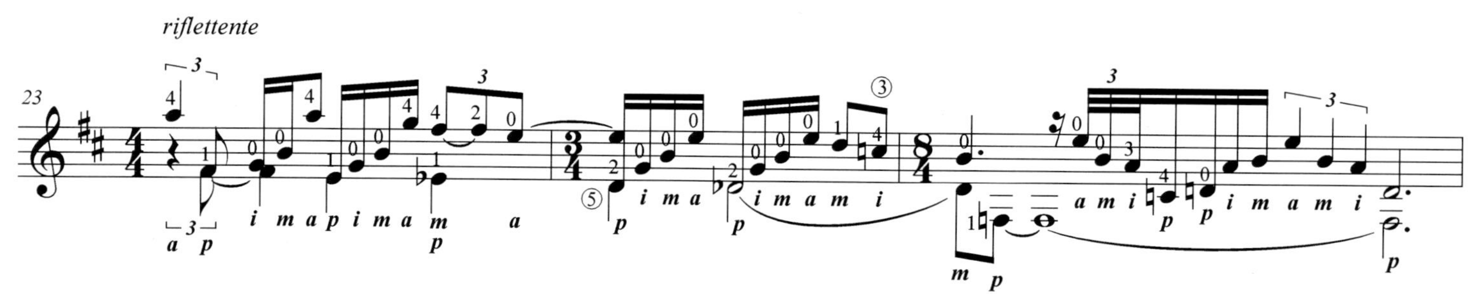
riflettente

26
29
agitato
mf
31
mf
33
mf
CV
f
CIV
35
mf
mp

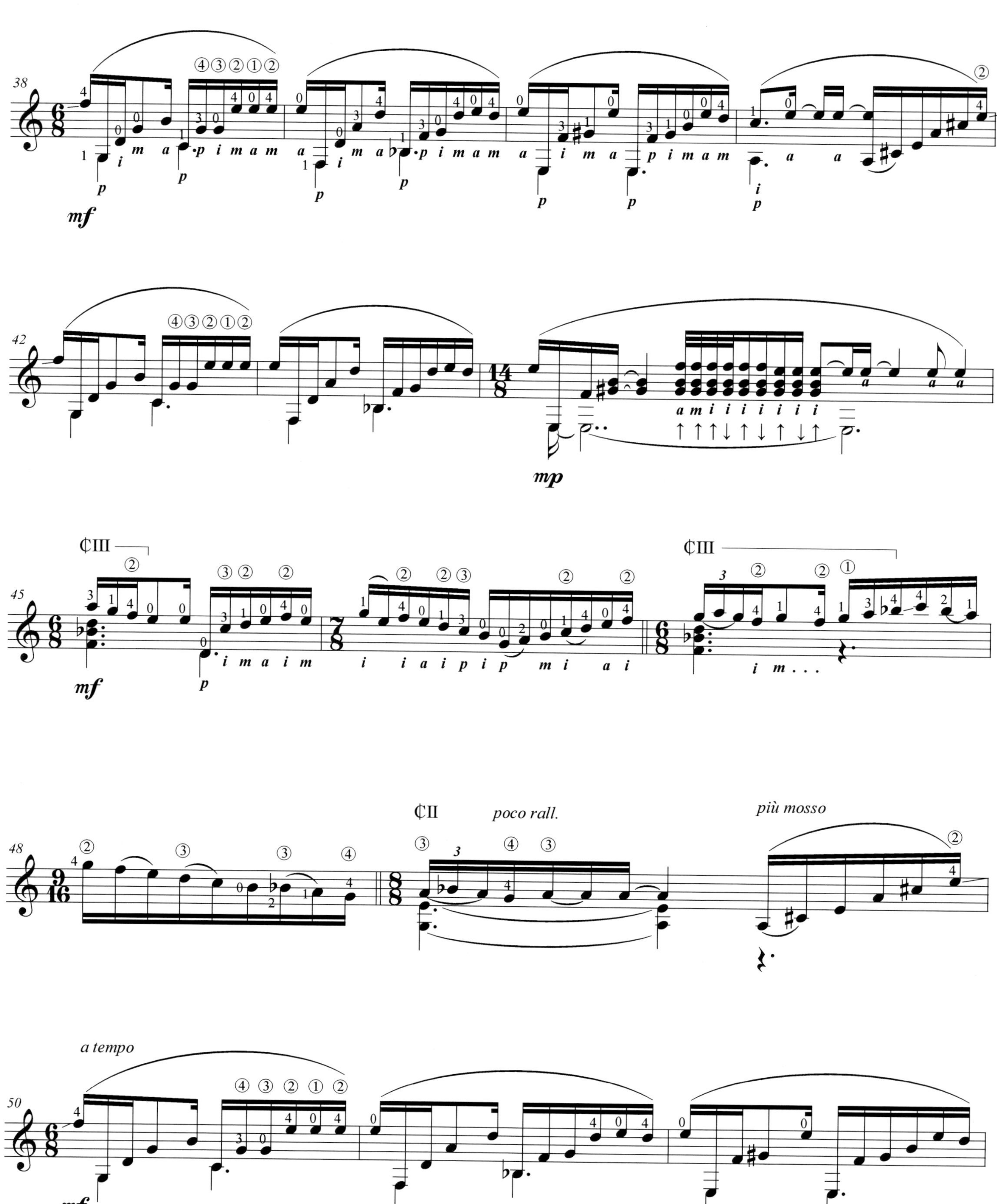
mf
mp
mf
poco rall.
più mosso
a tempo
mf

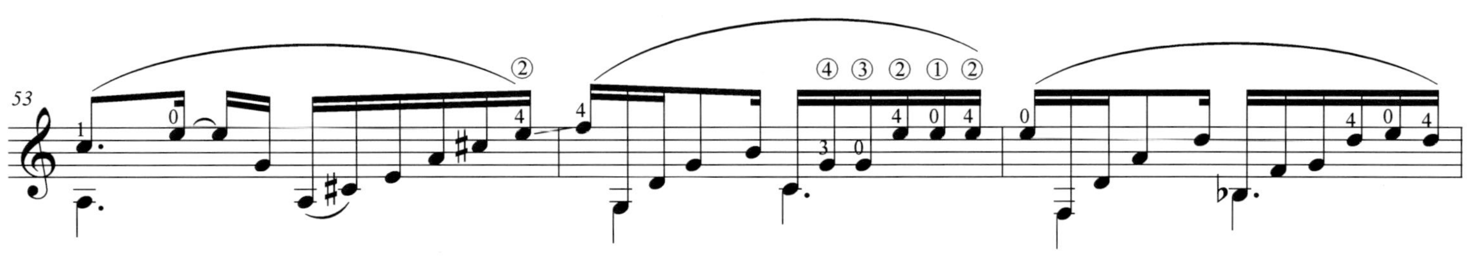
53

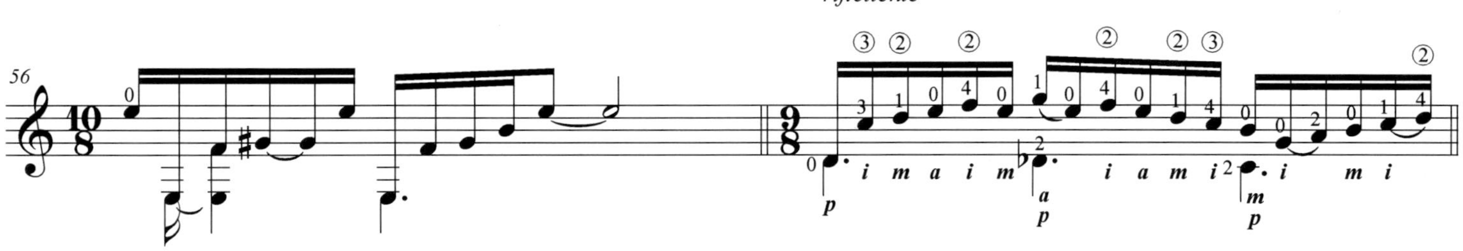
56
riflettente

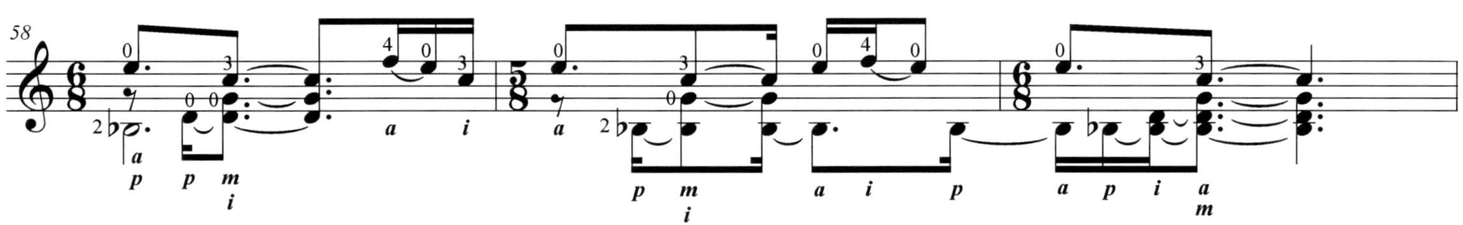
58

61
agitato
mf

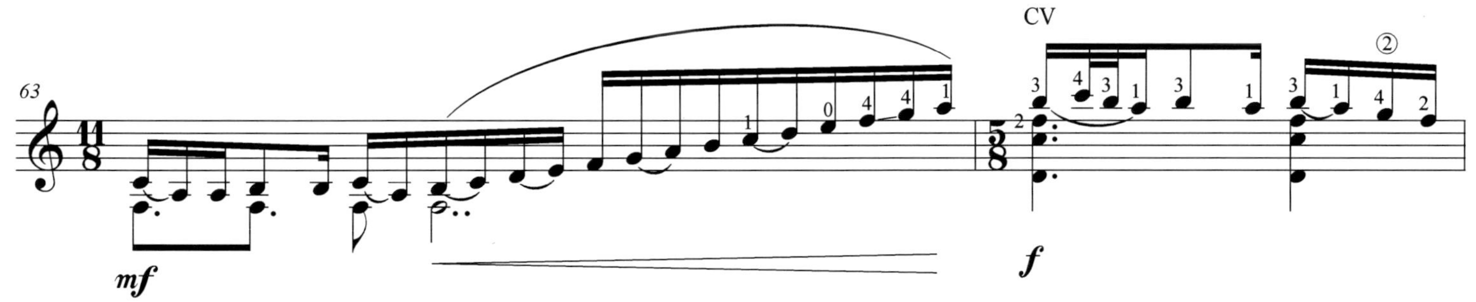
63
CV
mf
f

CIV
mf
riflettente

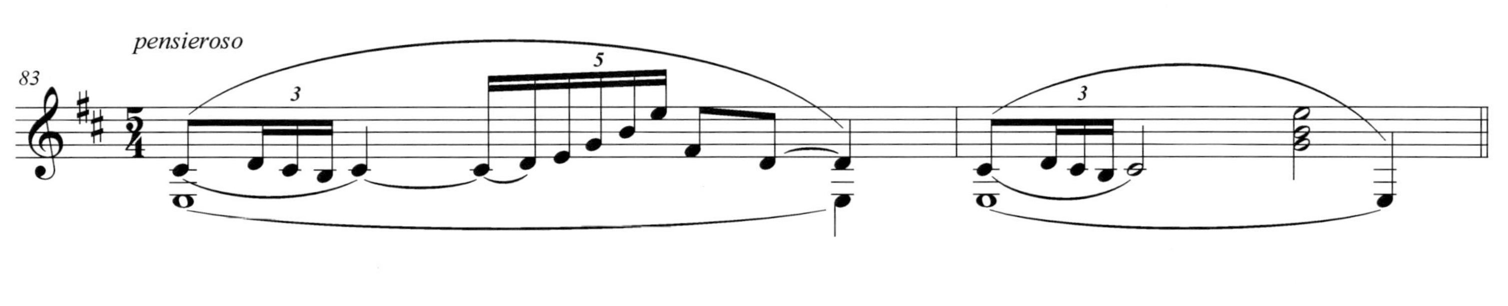
pensieroso
83

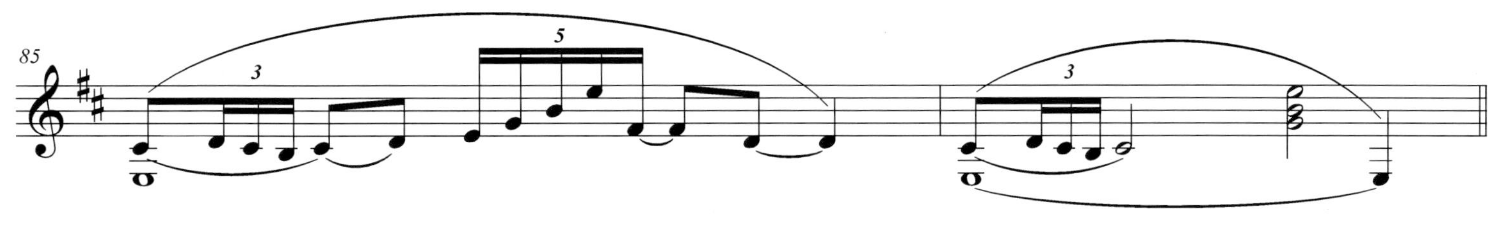
85

87
p

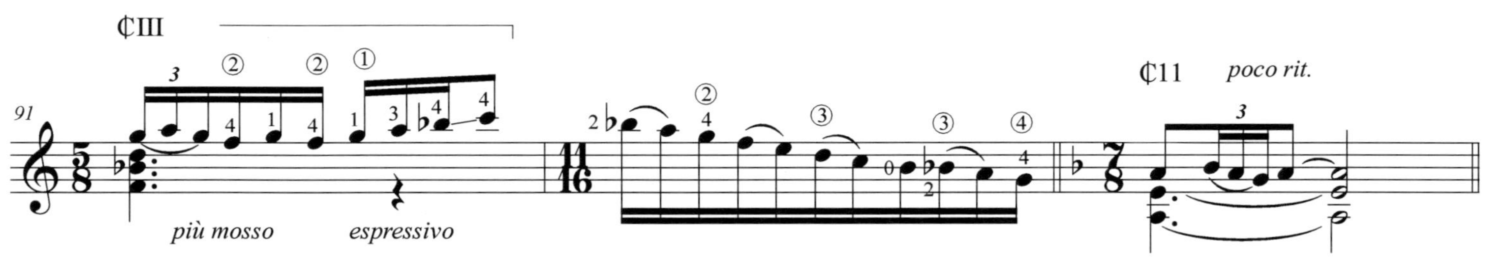
CIII
91
più mosso
espressivo
C11
poco rit.

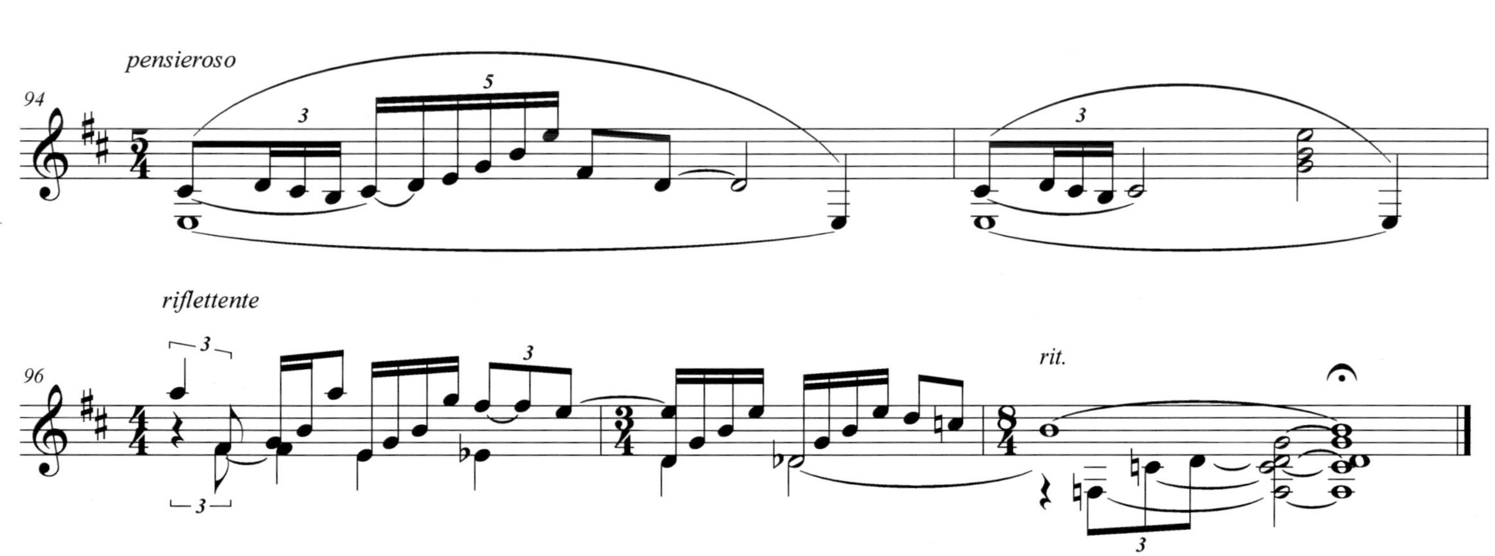
pensieroso
94
riflettente
96
rit.

Catnip

Capo II
6th to D *sempre legato throughout when possible*

Larry Hammett

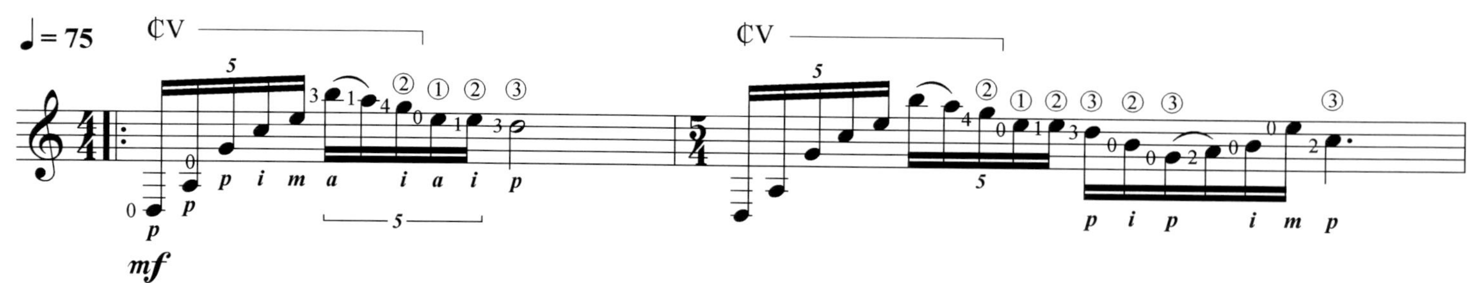

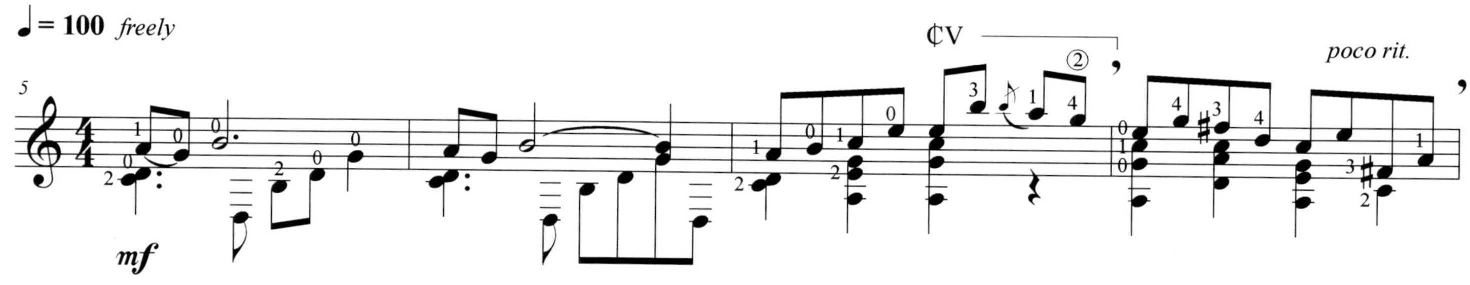

più mosso
rit.

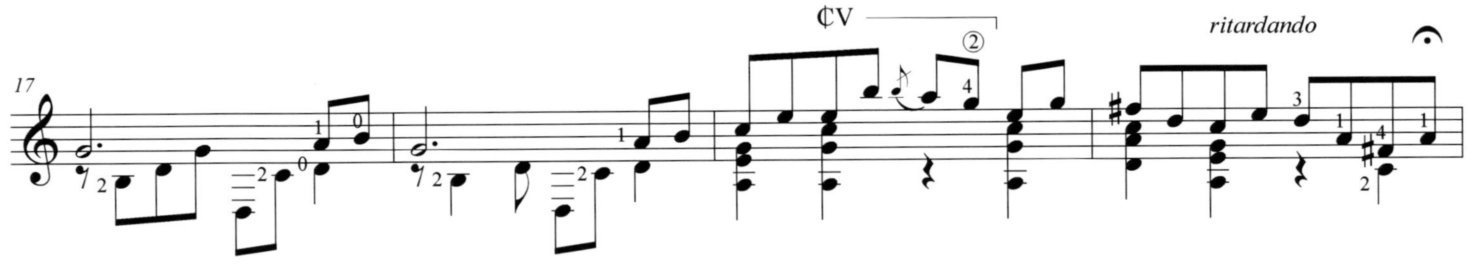
CV
ritardando

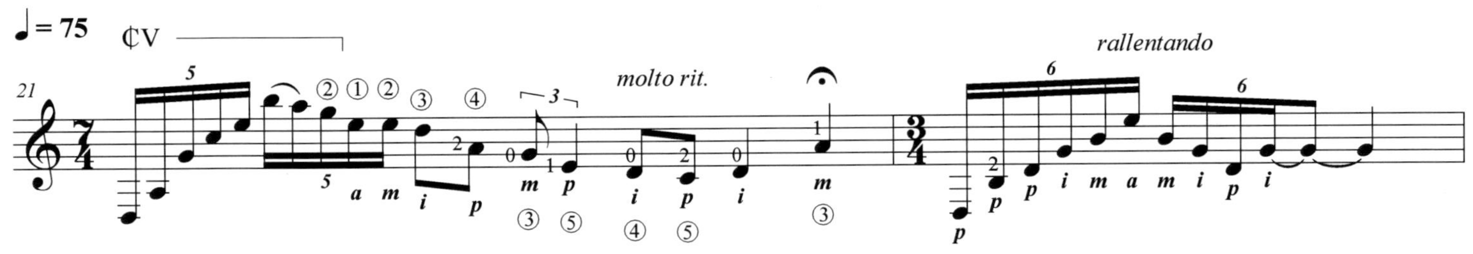
♩= 75
CV
molto rit.
rallentando

CV
più mosso
mf

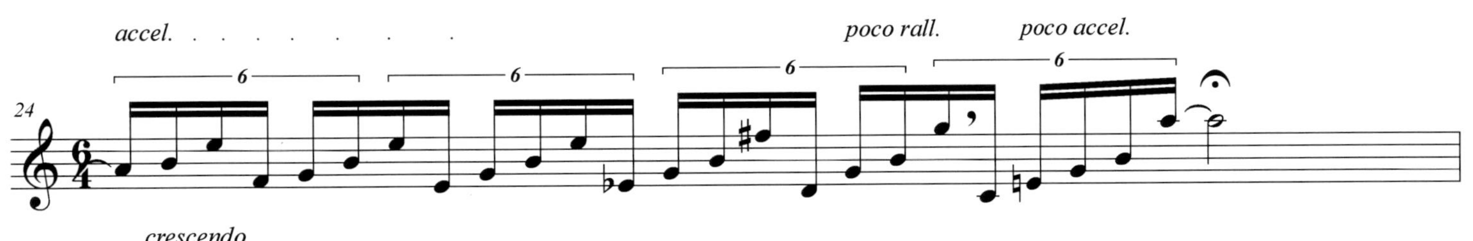
accel.
poco rall.
poco accel.
crescendo

♩= 100 freely
CV
poco rall.
mf

più mosso
poco rall.
mf

più mosso
poco rall.
mf

CV
rallentando
mf

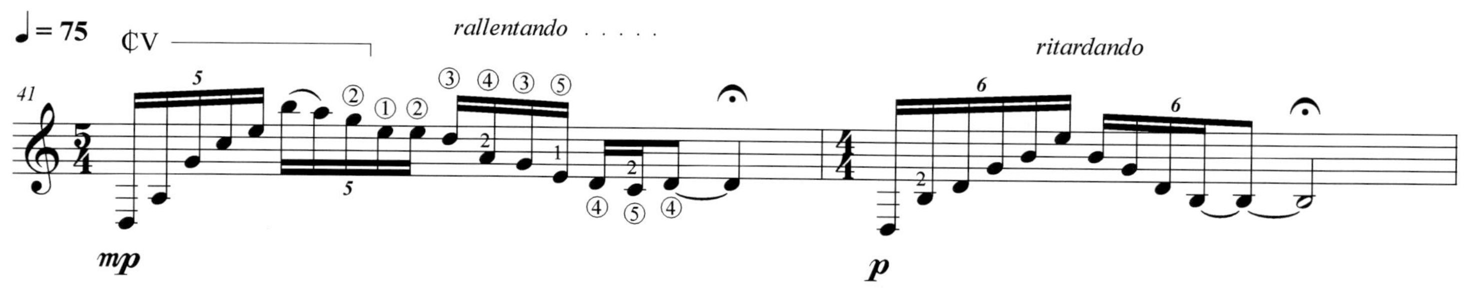

♩= 75
CV
rallentando . . . . .
ritardando
mp
p

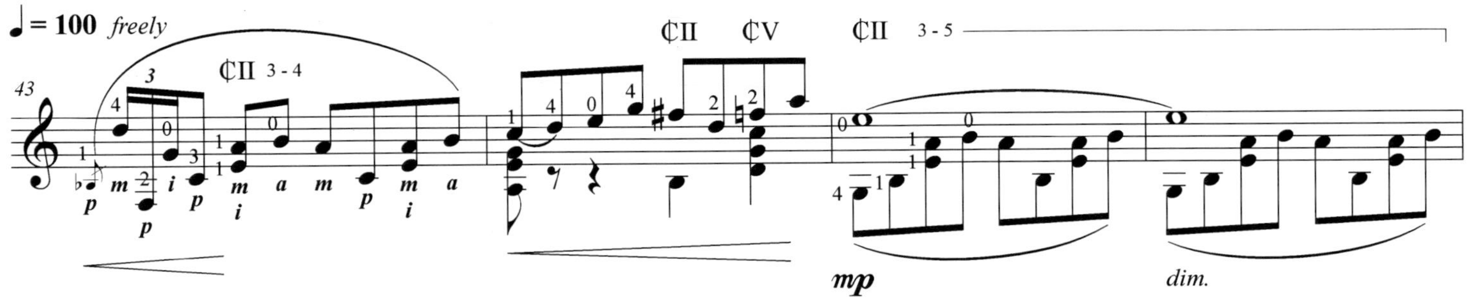
♩ = 100 freely
43
CII 3 - 4
CII
CV
CII 3 - 5
mp
dim.

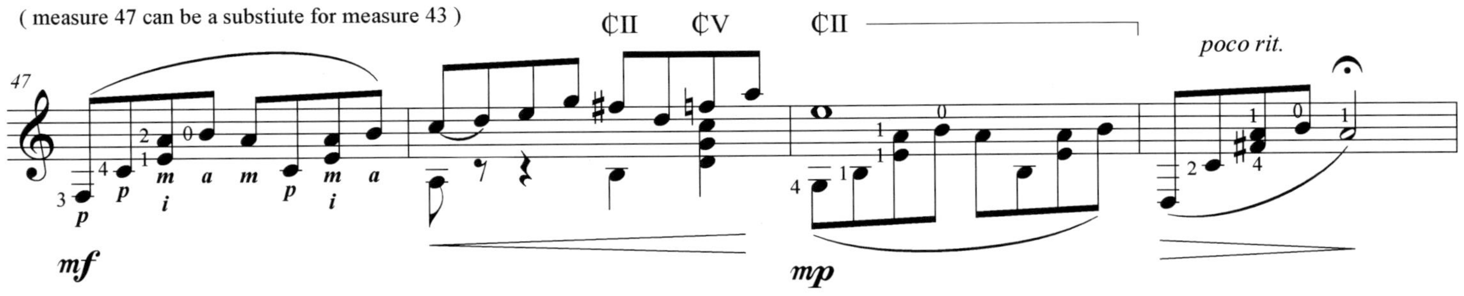
(measure 47 can be a substiute for measure 43)
47
CII
CV
CII
poco rit.
mf
mp

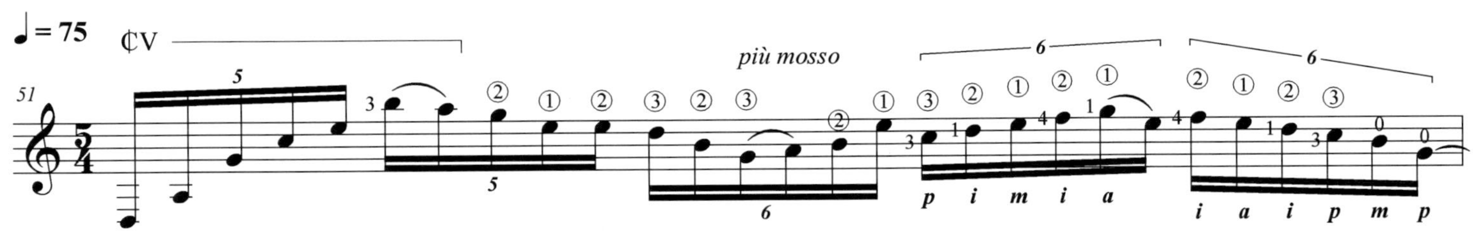
♩ = 75
CV
51
più mosso

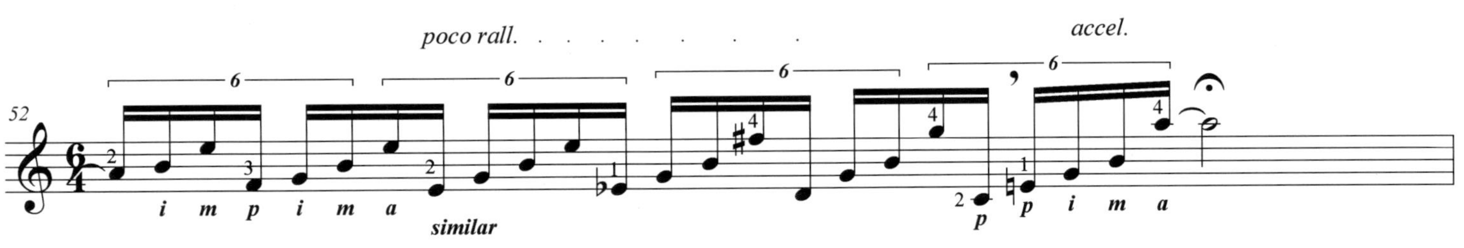
52
poco rall. . . . .
accel.
similar

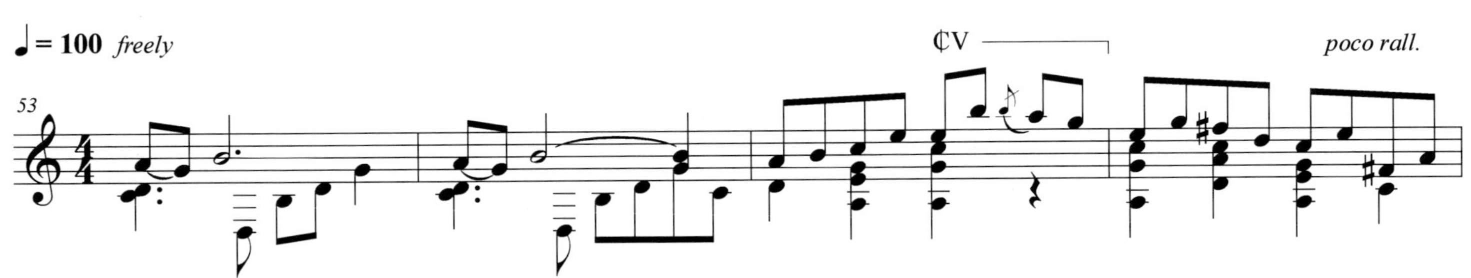
♩ = 100 freely
53
CV
poco rall.

a tempo
57
più mosso
poco rall.

più mosso
61
poco rall.
più mosso
¢V
poco rall.

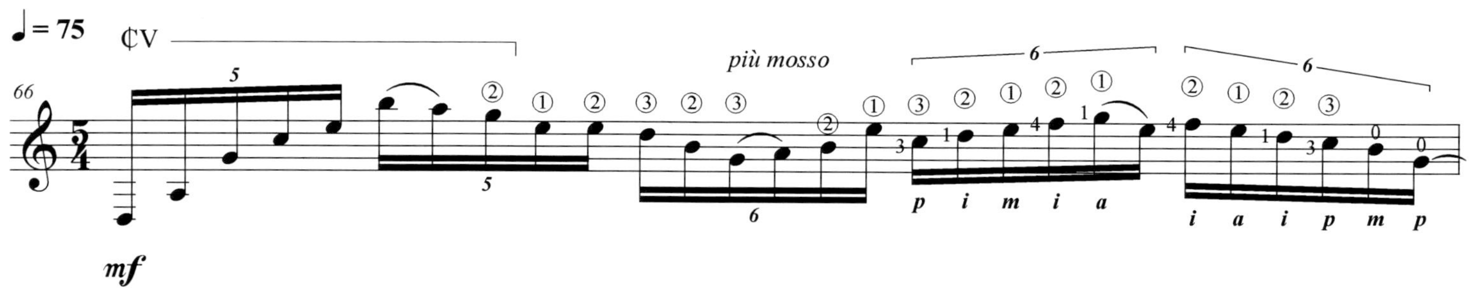
♩ = 75
¢V
66
più mosso
p i m i a
i a i p m p
mf

accel.
poco rall. . . . .
67
i m p i m a
similar
p p i m a

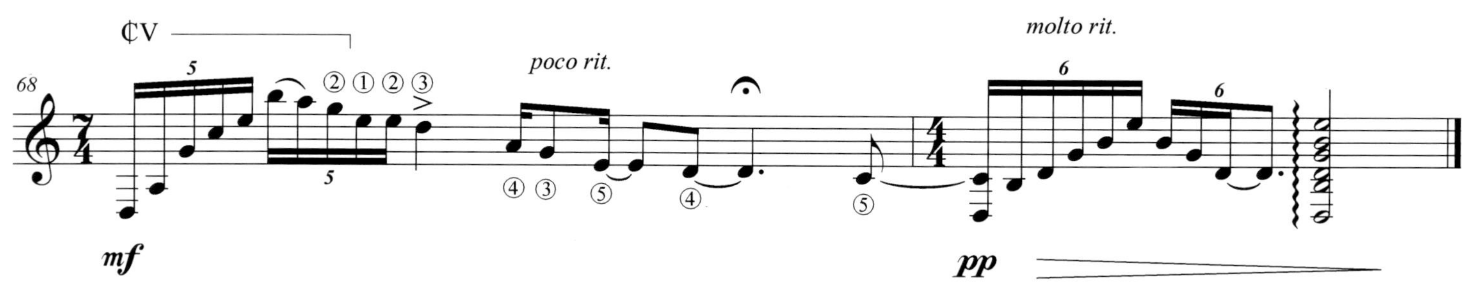
¢V
68
poco rit.
molto rit.
mf
pp

This page has been left blank to avoid an awkward page turn.

Purrrrrrr

5th string to G
6th string to C

Larry Hammett

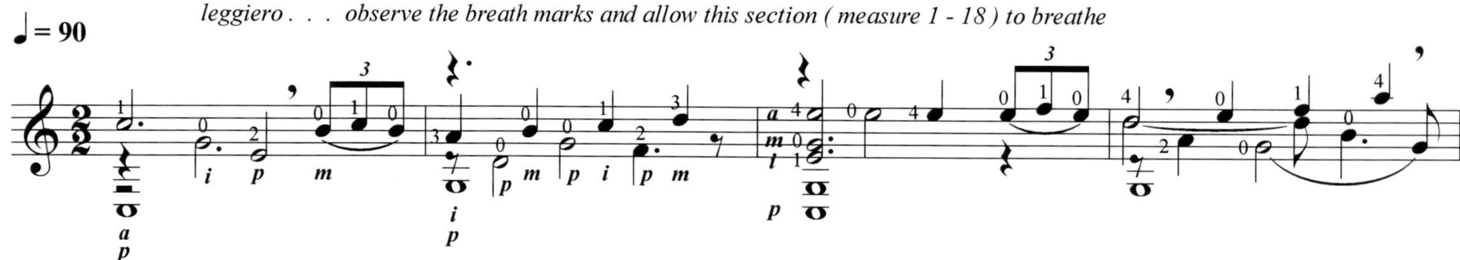

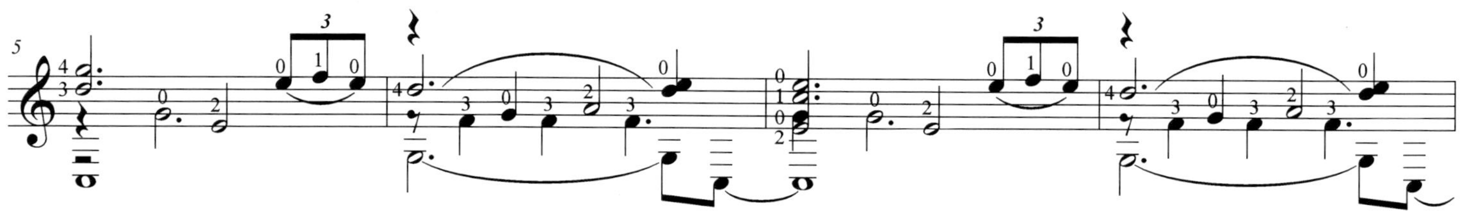

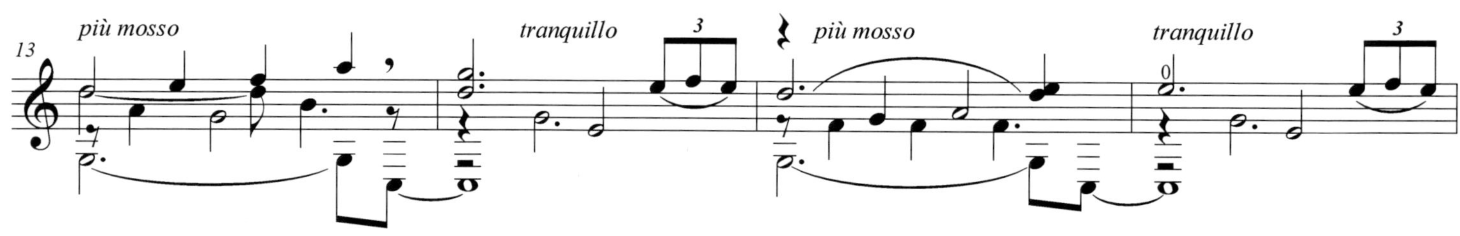

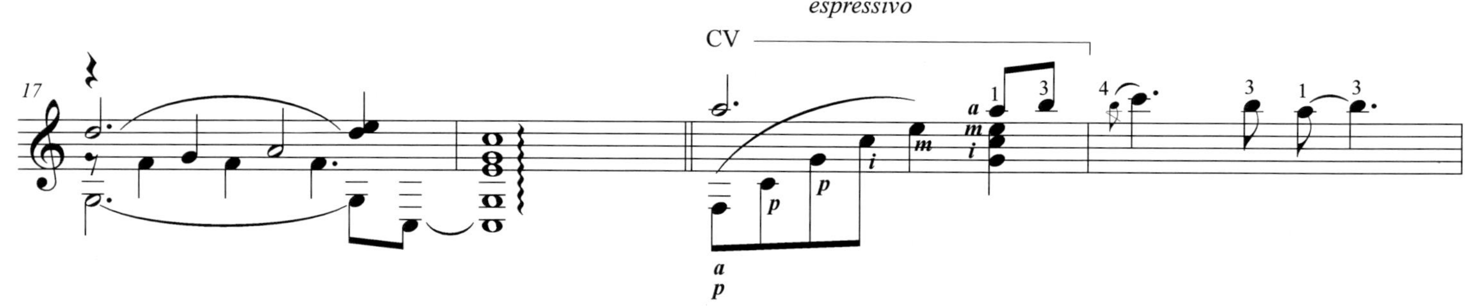

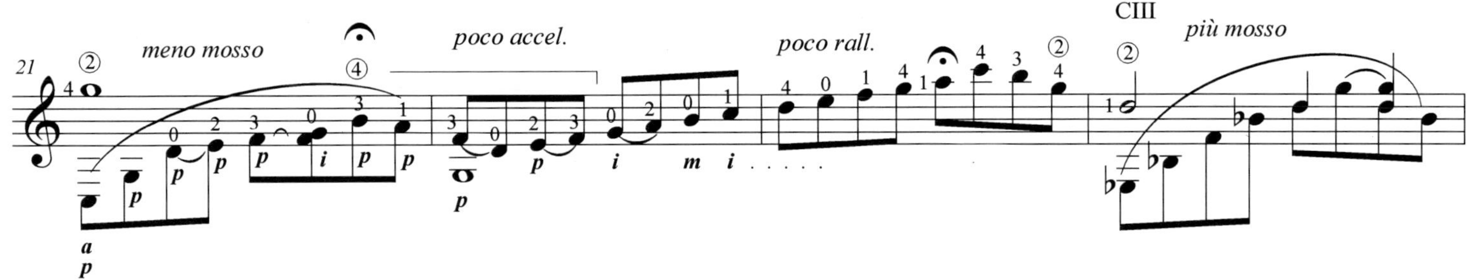
meno mosso
poco accel.
poco rall.
CIII
più mosso

CI
più mosso
poco rit.
CV
similar

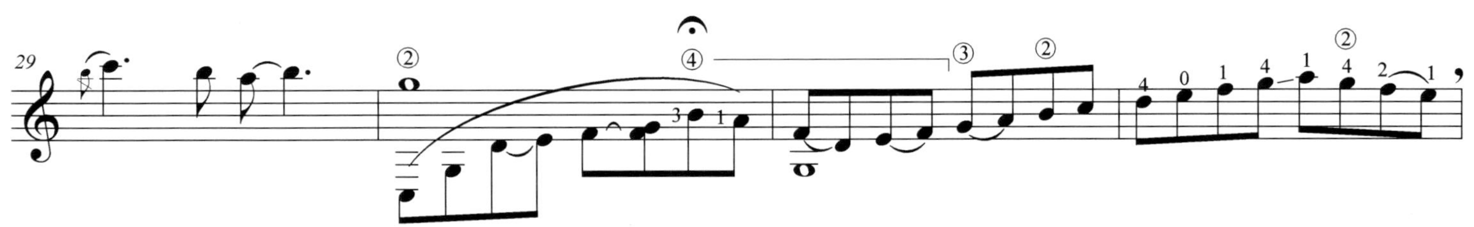

CIII
più mosso
CI
meno mosso
ritardando

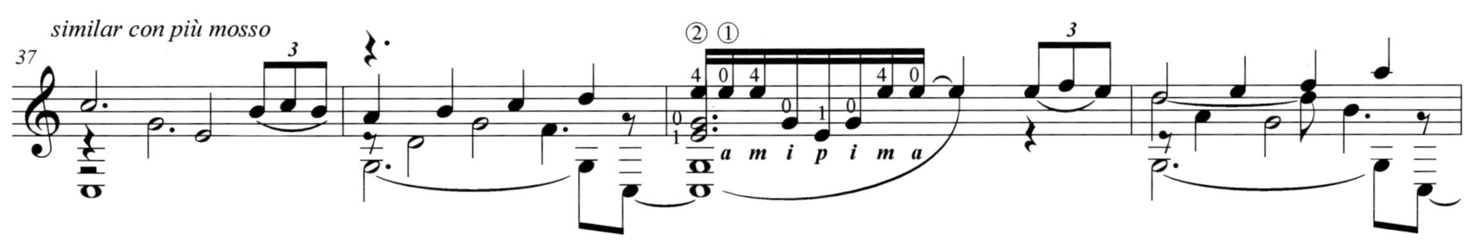
similar con più mosso

41

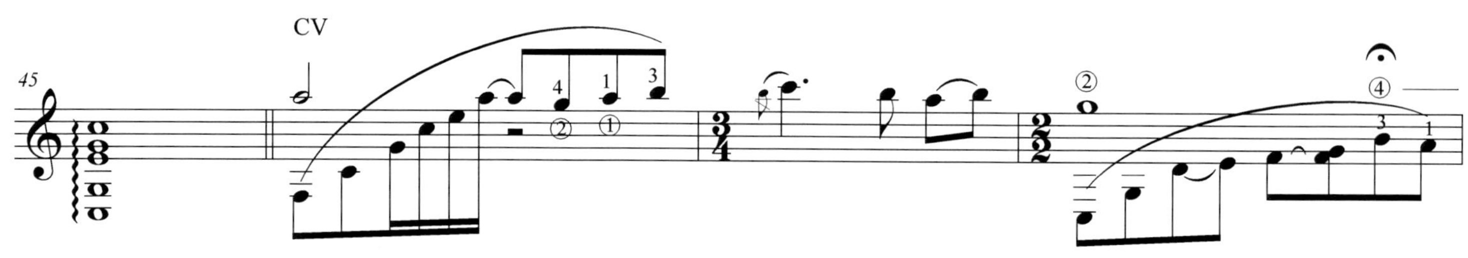
45
CV

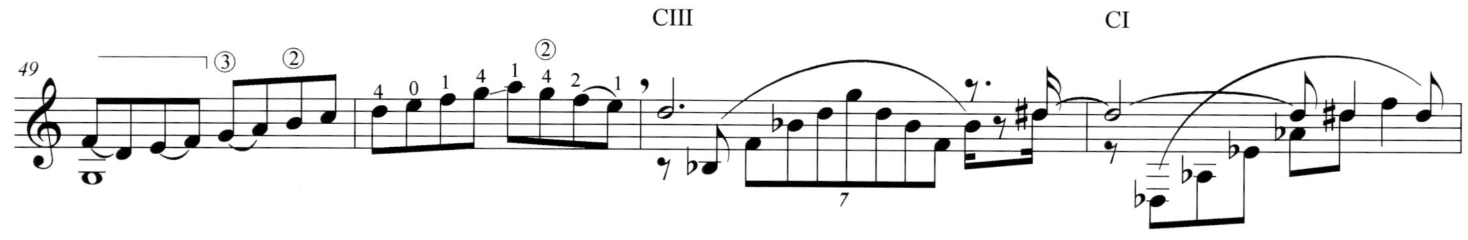
49
CIII
CI

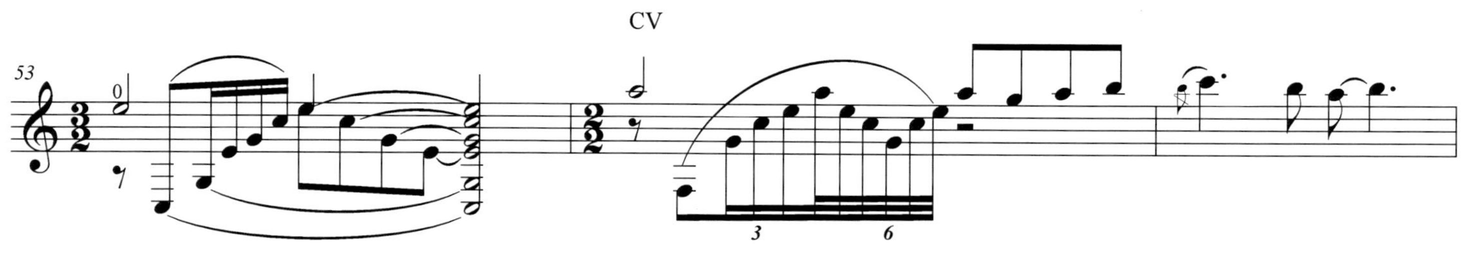
53
CV

56
meno mosso
poco accel.
rall.
CIII

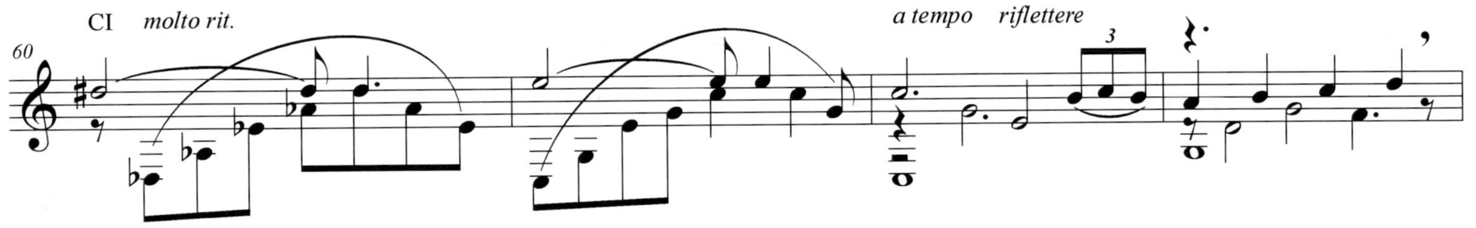
CI
molto rit.
a tempo
riflettere

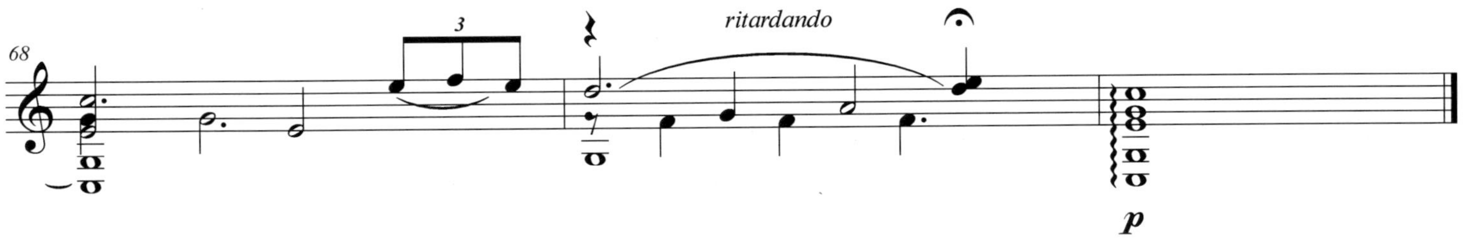
ritardando

La Gata

Capo II

Larry Hammett

Light and free with a slight sense of urgency

♩= 100

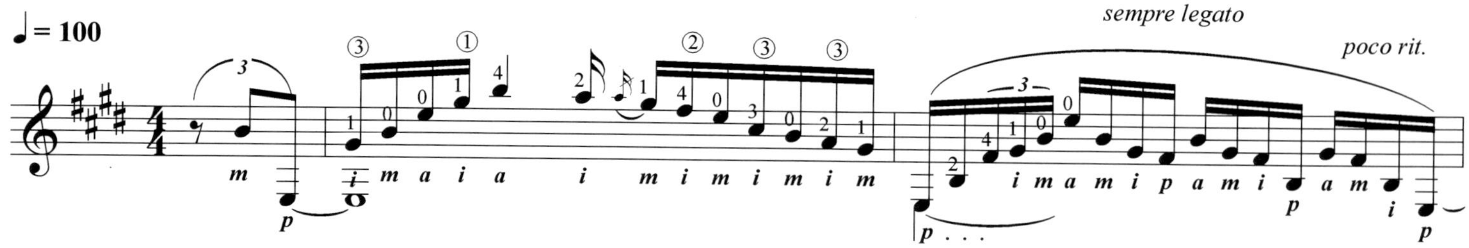

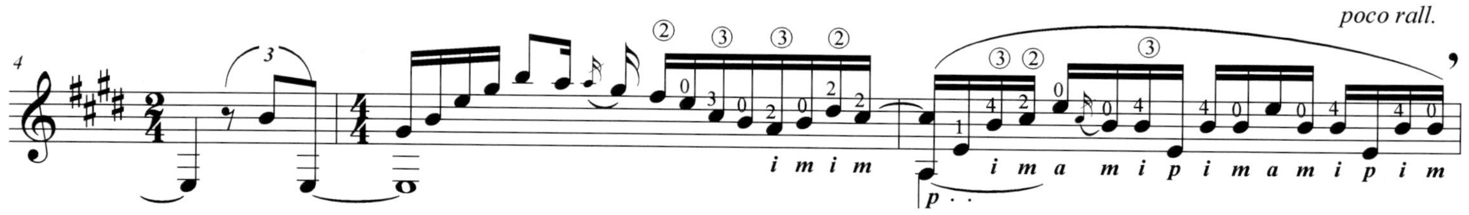

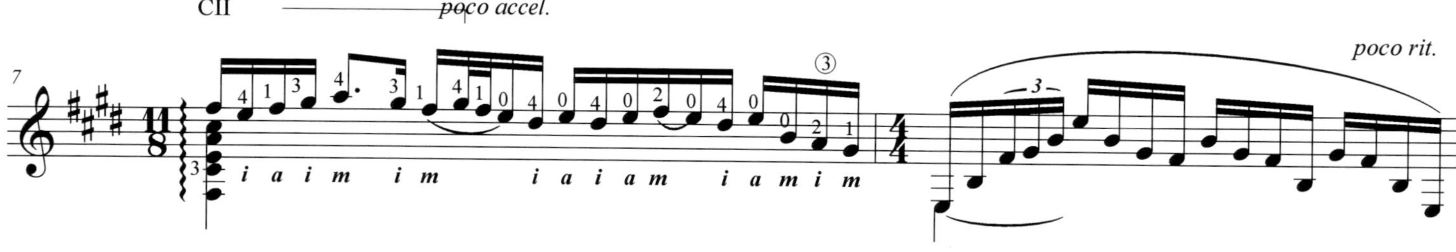

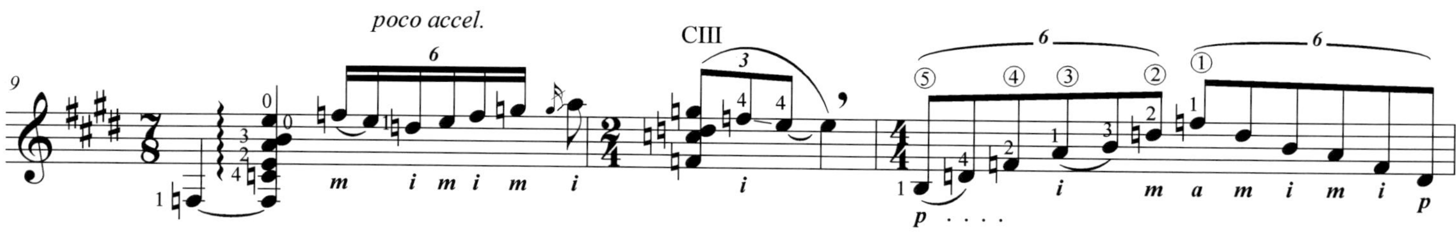

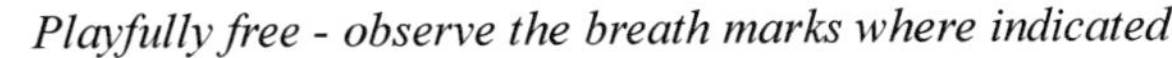
Playfully free - observe the breath marks where indicated

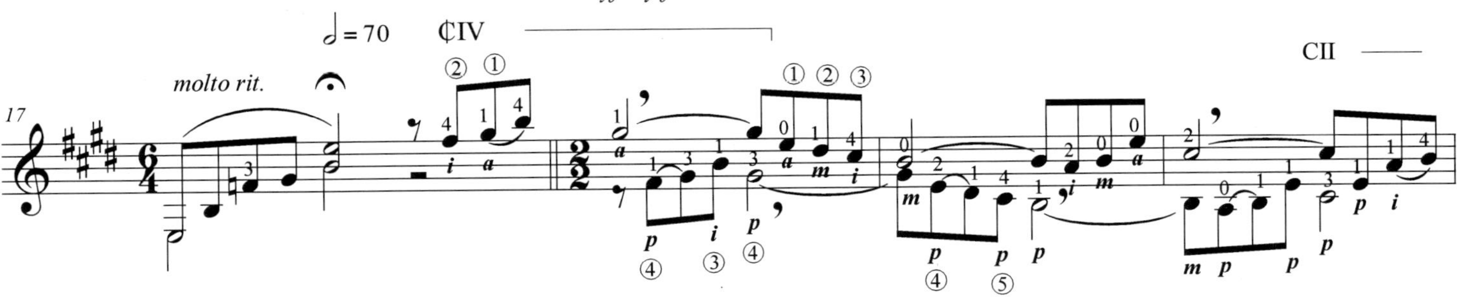
molto rit.
= 70
ȻIV
CII

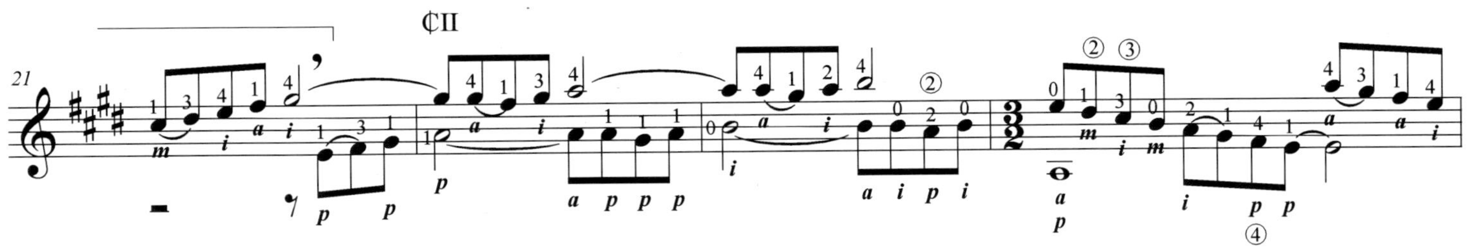
ȻII

a piacere
ȻII
poco rall.

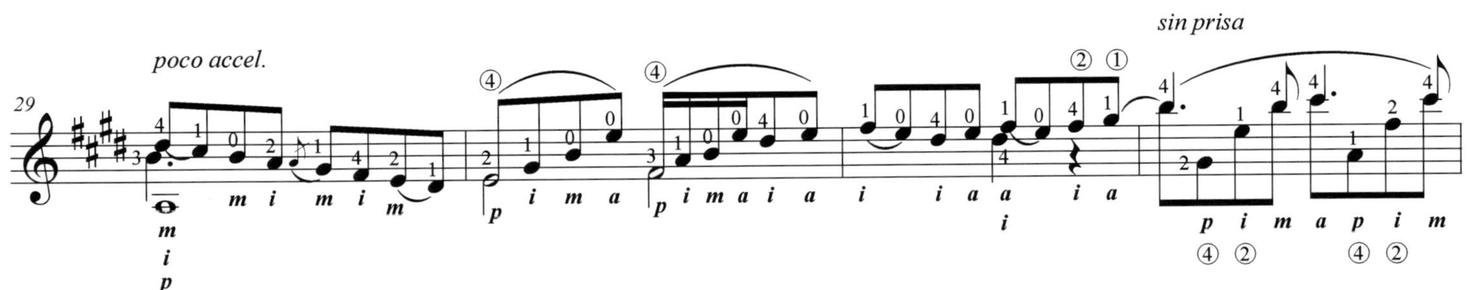
poco accel.
sin prisa

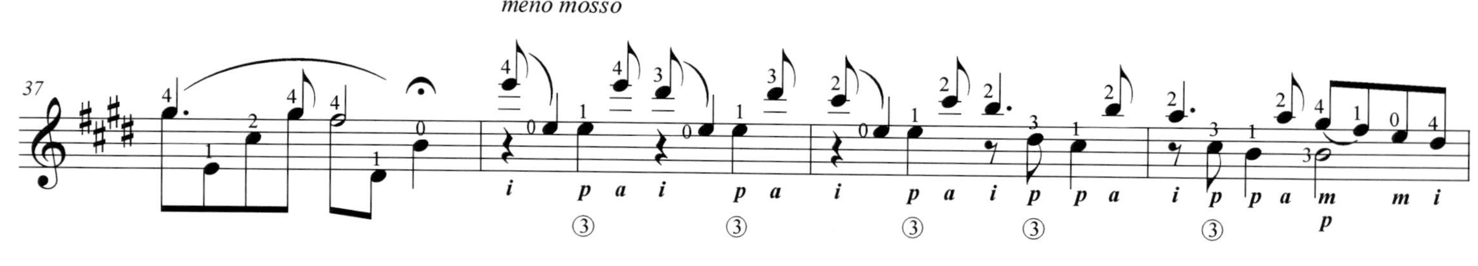
meno mosso
i p a i p a i p a i p p a i p p a m m i
p

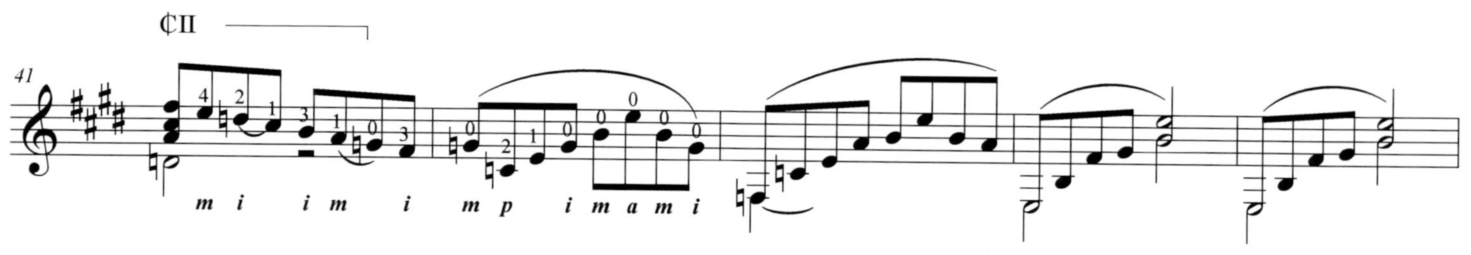
CII
m i i m i m p i m a m i

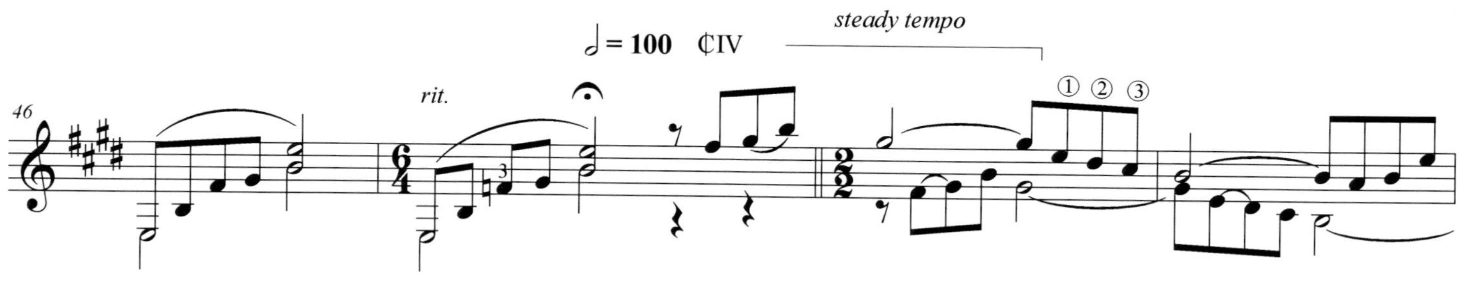
rit.
= 100 CIV
steady tempo

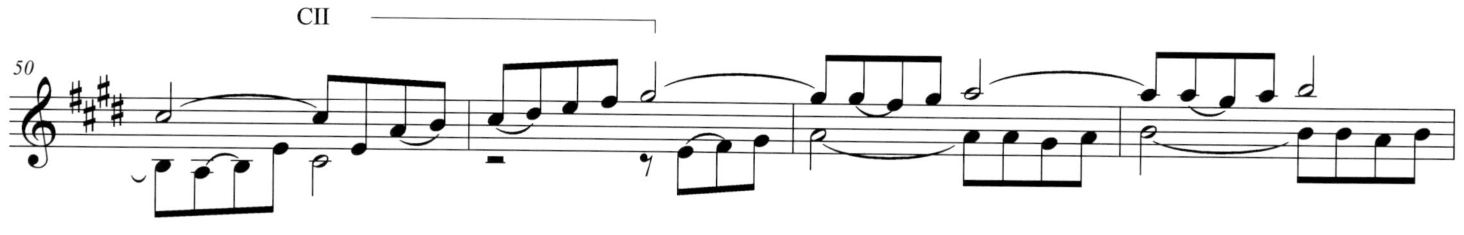
CII

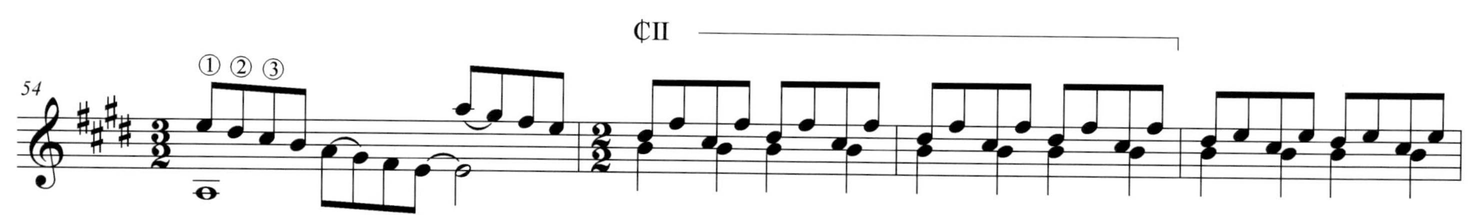
CII

rit.
rit.
pp

El Fin de Novena Vida

Capo II
6th string to D

Larry Hammett

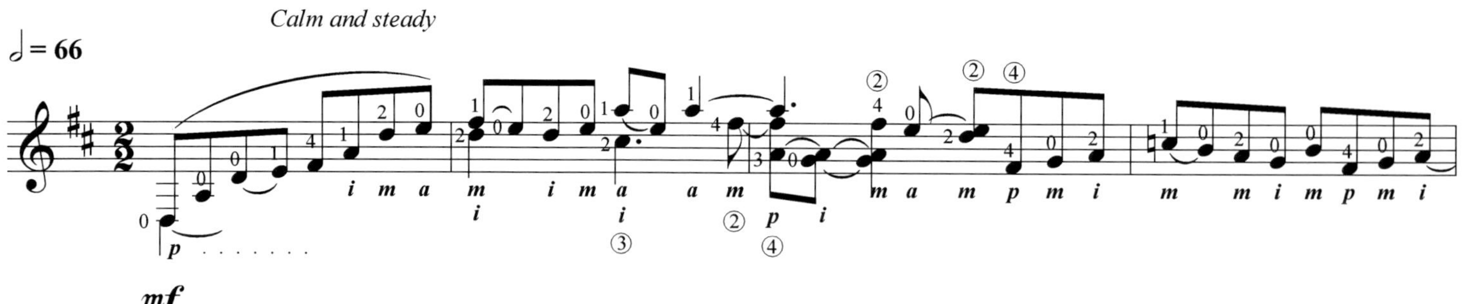

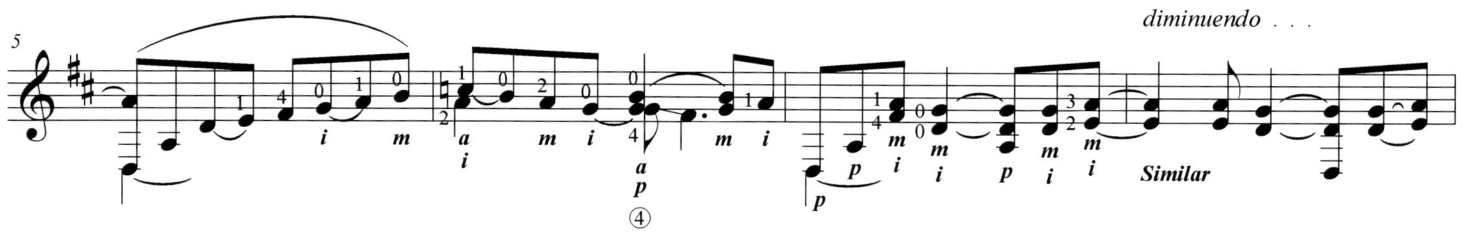

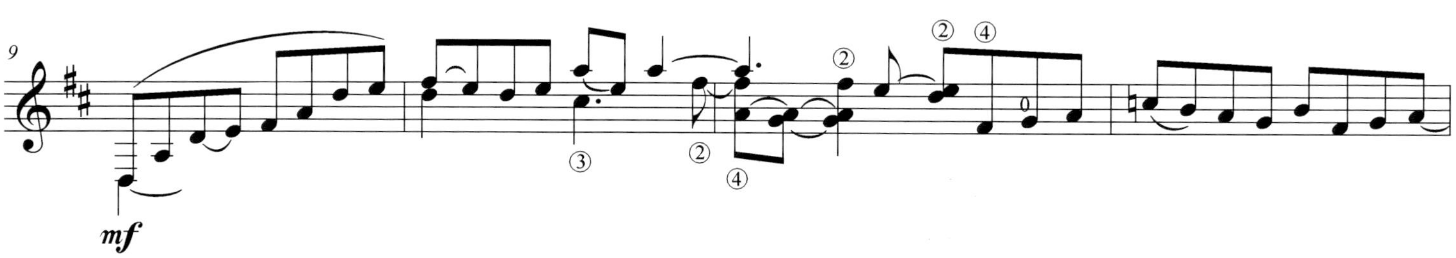

long diminuendo with no ritardando

About the Composer

Larry Hammett is a guitarist, producer, composer and educator. His principal genre is impossible to classify, as his resume of recordings and performances include classical, jazz, pop, avantgarde, blues, country, bluegrass, flamenco, Balkan and, more generally, world music. As an ambassador of the guitar, Hammett has performed and given master classes in France, Mexico, Argentina, Greece, Serbia, Turkey, Armenia, Spain and throughout the United States. In 2012, Hammett co-founded the Unlimited Music & Arts Festival in Vyzitsa, Greece and in 2018, the Paros International Guitar Festival on Paros island, Greece. As a composer, his six albums—*Brazos Island*, *The Larry Hammett Quartet*, *Fantasias Felinas*, *The Larry Hammett Quartet featuring Genie Jones*, *Musiques a Voir*, and *Live at the Grand House*—are aired world-wide and can be found on iTunes, Apple Music, Spotify, CD Baby, Digital Cable Radio, Pandora, and a host of other licensing organizations. In addition, his collaborative works include compositions for film, theater, and modern dance. As a producer and arranger, Hammett is highly regarded and has worked on projects throughout the world. He is currently the coordinator of guitar studies at The University of Oklahoma where he has been since joining the faculty in 1991.